Out of ⊙ Control

by MARK LOWRY

WORD PUBLISHING
Dallas•London•Vancouver•Melbourne

OUT OF CONTROL
by Mark Lowry

Unless otherwise indicated, Scripture quotations used in this book
are from the King James Version of the Bible (KJV).

References indicated NKJV are from the New King James Version.
Copyright © 1979, 1980, 1982, 1992, Thomas Nelson, Inc., Publisher.
References indicated NIV are from the New International Version.
Copyright © 1973, 1978, 1984 International Bible Society.
Used by permission of Zondervan Bible Publishers.

This book is a work of outrageous humor. Names, characters, places, and
incidents are either the product of the author's gross exaggeration and imagination, or are used fictitiously. Any resemblance to actual events, locales,
organizations, or persons, living or dead, is entirely coincidental and beyond
the intent of either the author or the publisher.

ISBN 0-8499-1300-4

Printed in the United States of America

OUT OF CONTROL

Table of Contents
(Contents may have settled during shipping.)

5

Life as a Profound Philosopher (or Hey, I needed a Section for My Really Deep Thoughts)

With All My Liver

The Plumber's Coming in the Morning

Life Backwards

Well Worshiping

Relatively Perfect

A Fate Worse Than Death

Takin' Time to Be Thankful

Since I've Given Up Hope

Shrimp Nightmares

Are You Lonely Tonight?

Alarm-Clock Faith

Can't Fail

Looking Forward

Let's All Be Heels

etc.

THE LAST WORD
   (Mama finally gets it.)

APPENDIX (Sorry, had it removed)

INDEX

OUTDEX

BIBLE MAPS

AUTOGRAPH PAGE (Have people who didn't sign your yearbook sign here.)

BLANK PAGES TO FILL UP SPACE

BOOK COVER JACKET PHOTO (Objects in picture are MUCH bigger than they appear.)

Mark My Word

You're Out of Control, Young Man!

That's pretty much the anthem that all the adults I have known have been singing in unison all my life. Hey, all I know is that what I used to get a whipping for, I now get paid for.

And look at this, I'm even getting paid for it to be put into print. **Look at me, Mama! I'm a book author!**

I hope Miss Barth, my sixth-grade teacher, gets a copy of this book. She thought I'd grow up one day and become a mass murderer or something.

I also hope it's noticed by Mr. Pickering, one of my college professors, who scolded me one day in my television and film class for looking in the camera and mouthing, "Hi Mom!" That's all I did, "Hi Mom!" I didn't even say it out loud, I just mouthed it. But he wanted everyone to be perfect, so maybe mouthing was enough. And my history professor, Mr. Rambo, whom I told I didn't

1

have time to study history, I was too busy making it! He was not amused.

Well, here it is . . .
Miss Barth . . .
Mr. Pickering . . .
Mr. Rambo . . .

MY FIRST BOOK!

And yes, I'm still out of control. Being in control is not fun. And life is too short for everything not to be a blast. You know, we're going to be dead a long time. We'll have plenty of time to "be still." While we're here we need to live, live, live, and that involves movement. A friend of mine once said to me, "Mark, you need to slow down and smell the roses." I said, "I've smelled roses, and they all smell alike. You've smelled one rose, you've smelled them all." Don't get me wrong. I love the smell of roses, but there's more to life than roses. There are thorns to experience too.

I look at life like a journey. You know, planning a vacation is a lot more fun than doing it. I've always looked forward to doing things. I'm not saying this is the right way, but it's my way. I've made it thirty-something years trying to soak up as much of this life as I can. I think God expects us to live life to the fullest. Milk it dry! When I get to the end of my journey, I won't be able to say I did everything right. I'll probably wish I had done some things differently.

But I do wanna be able to say, "What a trip!"

FIRST
HALF

Life with
Mama

My Mama, the Screamer

I grew up in church.

My daddy was a church deacon, my mother was a church pianist, and I was the church brat.

And I wasn't just your normal brat. When people met me, they knew why some animals eat their young.

I had airbags on my baby buggy, I was so hyperactive.

I was so hyperactive that the minute I learned to walk, Mama pointed me toward the door.

I was so bad I was sent to a psychiatrist in the third grade. The principal of my school actually told my mother that I needed psychiatric help.

So one day Mama told me, "Mark, you've been chosen out of your whole school to get to go and take some tests."

I said, "Well, hot dog, Mama, let's go."

The psychiatrist ran these tests on me. She was a very nice lady. She asked me questions about my mom, my dad, and my older brother, Mike, who's perfect.

Perfect people have no right to live. My brother never did anything wrong. He was so perfect, we used his halo as a night-light. It was sickening.

She didn't ask about my little sister, because she wasn't born yet. Melissa came along nine years after I did. Mama told me later she waited nine years between us because she was scared to death she was going to have another one like me. But Melissa turned out to be just like my brother. Perfect.

The psychiatrist finished all of her tests on me, went out in the lobby, and told my mother, "Mrs. Lowry, your boy Mark is normal."

"WHAT?!" said Mama.

Mama didn't believe that. So she took me to another doctor to get a second opinion. That doctor ran an EEG on my brain. That's a test where they tape wires to your head. I thought they were trying to electrocute me.

But that test came up normal, too. Mama was frustrated.

But Daddy wasn't frustrated. Daddy found a scripture in Proverbs that says, "Foolishness is bound up in the heart of a child; [but] the rod of correction will drive it far from him."

That changed my life. Daddy started taking God at his word and beating the devil out of me every night.

Don't get me wrong. Dad is not a child abuser. Dad is the godliest guy I've ever known. My dad never hollers, never yells, never screams, never tells you to do anything twice. He's always about an inch from a coma.

He doesn't even scream at football games. He just sits there. If he gets real excited about the game, he'll make this sucking sound on the back of his front teeth.

It sounds like this: "Thphtttttttttt." ✘

And that meant he was on the verge of a heart attack.

It was the same thing at home. When I, the brat, would push him too far, he didn't holler, yell, or scream. He'd just make that sound:

"Thtttttph."

You could stand right next to him when he made that sound, and you probably wouldn't even hear it.

I could hear it a block away.

When Dad went "Thpphhttt," I knew my party was over.

Mama, of course, is the opposite of my dad.

Where Dad is calm, cool, and collected, Mama can't even spell "calm, cool, and collected."

✘(Hear the true-to-life sound effect preserved for posterity on my "For the First Time on Planet Earth" CD, available at finer Christian bookstores and bargain basements EVERYWHERE).

Mama is a SCREAMER.

Do you know what a SCREAMER is?

A SCREAMER is someone you don't pay any attention to—that is, until she hits a certain pitch. And you know she's hit that certain pitch when garage doors fly open all over the neighborhood.

She used to look at me and say, "MARK! You just wait till your dad comes home!"

My dad *always* came home.

He'd walk through the door from work, and the first thing he'd hear is my mother screaming:

"CHARLES, YOU'VE GOT TO TALK TO MARK!"

And he'd go:

"Thtttttph."

I remember one time when I was eight and my brother was ten; I was in the kitchen minding my own business. My brother Mike, Mr. Perfect, came walking through the kitchen with that look on his face.

Have you ever seen anyone with that look? It's a look that says, "I need to be slapped."

So what was I to do? I walked over and slapped him.

The next thing I knew, I was on the floor wrestling with Mr. Perfect. He had me by the throat; I was pounding him in the face. We were having a wonderful time.

That is, until Mama had enough.

She said that a lot.

"MARK, I'VE JUST ABOUT HAD ENOUGH."

I'd say, "Well, Mama, help yourself, there's plenty more."

There came a day when I got too big to whip. By the time I was fifteen, she'd be spanking me on my rear end, and I'd be looking at my watch. Or I'd say, "Ooh, a little more to the left."

Mama didn't like that.

But I wasn't too big to spank this particular day. And while we were having a great time knocking over kitchen chairs and bouncing off the kitchen table, Mama was in the kitchen, too, washing dishes. We hardly knew she was there.

Until, that is, Mama had enough.

I wish that God would build on the back of every mother's head a little red light that would start flashing ten seconds before "enough." You can make a lot of tracks in ten seconds.

But we got no warning that morning. And before we knew what happened, Mama had thrown herself over the kitchen sink, and this is what we heard:

"I'VE FAILED! I'VE FAILED! I'VE FAILED! LORD, FORGIVE ME FOR FAILING WITH THESE BOYS!"

My brother and I quit fighting and started watching. This was a lot better than fighting. Mama was pitching a fit.

"I'VE FAILED! I'VE FAILED!" she kept wailing, tears splashing off her cheeks.

Then, all of a sudden, the phone started ringing.

My brother and I stared at the phone then back at Mama. Then at the phone and back at Mama.

But she didn't even let up.

"I'VE FAILED! I HAVE FAILED!" she kept screeching.

9

I remember thinking, "I wonder who's going to get the phone? It sure wasn't going to be my brother or me."

And that left Mama. And she sure was in no condition to answer the phone. Her eyes were all red and puffy, tears were pouring down her face, and nothing but big, wailing sobs were coming out of her mouth.

Yet without slowing up a lick on the wailing, she turned and started walking toward the ringing phone.

I immediately started fasting and praying.

"Oh, Dear God, please don't let that be Daddy on the phone. God, I'll go to Africa, I'll wear polyester Bermuda shorts for the rest of my life. God, I'll marry a woman with a monkey on her head. Don't let that be Daddy on the phone."

Mama, still walking toward that phone, had moved into Phase Two.

"I can't BELIEVE the way you boys TREAT me (sob, honk, sniffle)!" Mama screeched as she raised her arm to the phone.

"I went through the VALLEY OF THE SHADOW OF DEATH to give you birth!" Mama bawled as she gripped the phone's receiver.

"Between the TWO OF YOU, I've been in LABOR HALF MY LIFE (honk, sniffle)!" Mama whined as she lifted the receiver from its cradle. "PUSH is more than just a sign on a door for ME!"

But then, just as the receiver got to her ear—

"And you TREAT ME (sob) LIKE . . . !"

Mama's voice suddenly turned peaches and cream and sweet birds singing: "Hellllooooooooooooo?"

I still can't figure out how she did that.

All Mama Ever Wanted

When I was a kid, I got a lot of spankings. These days, there is a big controversy about whether or not kids should be spanked. Well, that controversy is about thirty years too late, because my dad never heard it.

When I was growing up, most of my spankings were because of—I know this is going to be hard for you to believe—my mouth.

I can hear your gasp of shock.

My mouth's main problem was sassing my mother. We'd start off with a disagreement, it would move on to an argument, and then it would end up with me sassing her.

I could never pass up a good line.

And at that point in the discussion, Mama would always tell me what she wanted out of life. ✗

Every time. Every day. Probably two or three times a day. She would say the same thing.

At the same point in our argument, at the moment my mouth would sass her, she'd tell me the only thing she truly wanted.

Mama didn't care about new houses. She didn't care about new cars or new clothes. She had everything but the one thing she wanted most.

All my mother wanted out of life was "The Last Word."

✗(Hey, what are you looking down here for?)

11

She'd say, "Mark, you had BETTER let me have the LAST WORD."

And to be fair, I tried to give her the last word. But something brilliant would always pop into my mind and be out of my mouth before I could stop it.

So since I never gave her that last word, I got those whippings.

The last whipping I got was when I was fifteen. I was skinny back then. I had acne. I was like a pimple-cream poster child. I had braces on my teeth before they were fashionable. My brother accused me of eating car antennas.

And I had grown too big for Mama.

It all began on the way to school one morning, when I sassed Mama.

I don't remember what it was about. But I know how it ended: "MARK, I'm going to tell your FATHER."

I was thinking, "Yeah, right. She'll forget."

She didn't.

I went on to school. That afternoon, I went to Driver's Ed. After Driver's Education, my dad would always pick me up. And naturally, I would always ask, "Can I drive to church?" Because we were always on our way to church. And this happened on a Wednesday. We were Baptists, and good Baptists went to Wednesday night prayer meeting. When the church doors were open, we were there. Daddy was a dictator. We did not have a vote every four years on who was gonna run the family. Daddy ran the family, and we went to church. If the preacher was going to wash the windows on Thursday night, we filled our pew and we watched him do it.

And don't think I didn't try to get out of going to

church, like any normal kid. Many times, I'd say, "Daddy, I'm too sick to go to church."

He'd say, "Throw up and prove it."

And if I couldn't throw up, I went to church.

And if I DID throw up, he'd say, "Now don't you feel better? Let's go to church."

And that is a very important part of this story, because I came out of Driver's Education thinking we were going to church like we had done for the past fifteen years I had been in that family.

I walked up to our car, and said, "Daddy, can I drive to . . . ?"

"Get in the car," he said, cutting me off.

And it was his God-voice:

GET IN THE CAR.

All of a sudden, I remembered what I had done. I started praying, "Oh, Lord Jesus, come quickly."

I got in the car. And Daddy said, "Mark, do you remember sassing your Mother this morning?"

"Yes sir."

"We're not going to church. I'm going to take you home and I'm going to half-kill you."

Have you ever been half-killed?

I started thinking, "What am I going to do? If we're skipping church to give me a whipping, it's going to be a DOOZY!"

For the whole thirty-minute drive home, I was desperately thinking, "What am I going to do? What am I going to do!"

And then a thought dawned on me. A college student had told me once, "Mark, the next time you get a spanking,

13

try 'mind over matter.' I learned it in college. Get a blanket and bite it. Bite the blanket. Concentrate on the blanket. And you won't even feel what your dad's doing down south."

When I was fifteen, I thought all college students were brilliant. Now I'm here to tell you, they ain't. This college girl was about three fries short of a Happy Meal, if you ask me.

Because my daddy didn't whip you anywhere near where you'd bite a blanket.

When we got home, Daddy said what he always said:

"Go upstairs and prepare for your spanking."

I still don't have any idea what that means.

That started with my older brother. When he got a spanking, he would go upstairs and he would prepare. He knew what it meant: Go into your room, cry, think about what you've done, ask God to forgive you, and try to figure out how you'll never do that again.

Nobody ever explained that to me. So I would always go up and prepare.

I'd put on seventeen pairs of underwear and pull my jeans over that. And Dad would come to whip his deformed-looking son.

This time, though, I thought, "Nope, that college student told me to bite the blanket, so that's what I'm gonna do."

I went upstairs, and for thirty minutes I crammed this fuzzy University of Houston blanket down my throat. Most of that blanket was in my digestive tract before Dad entered my room. The spread was hanging out of my mouth. I was into that blanket. Or, I should say, it was into me. If I was going to try mind over matter, I was going to do it right.

I heard Daddy coming up the steps.

It sounded like this:

Boom! Boom! Boom! Boom! Click! And C-R-E-E-E-E-A—A-K! (We've got big doors in Texas.)

Daddy walked over to me and said, "Mark, this is going to hurt me worse than it hurts you, son."

Every time he said it, I would think, "Well, if that's the case, let's trade places. I'm the one who needs the punishment, so let me beat the tar out of you for once." But I never said it.

And then I heard the sound that, to this day, puts goosebumps up and down my spine. You know the sound? It's the sound of a belt flying from your daddy's beltloops.

Bp-bp-bp-bp-bp-bp-bp. POW!

You hear that, and you know Judgment Time has come.

The worst part of that night's whipping wasn't the whipping. It was the advice that college student gave me. For three days, I coughed up furballs and picked fuzz out of my braces.

But I've got a plan. I can't wait until Mom and Dad come to live with me. Oh, what a day that will be! The day Mama moves in with me, I'm taking the car keys away from her. She'll say, "Well, Scott Davis lets his mother drive."

I'm going to look at her and say, "But I'm not Scott Davis. Now go clean up your room. It's a pig sty in there, young lady. Don't start crying or I'll give you something to cry about."

And just as she starts to answer me, I'm going to say, "Mama, you BETTER let me have the LAST WORD! ✗

It'll be a great day.

Mama's on Hold

My mama was always standing up for God. She could witness to a statue and lead it to Christ.

I can remember Mama going to the supermarket, witnessing to the cashier lady and having her on her knees while the line was winding around the milk department, past the Ding-Dongs and the Twinkies, and back again.

I used to say, "Mama, this place is open twenty-four hours a day! You can come back at three in the morning and lead the whole place to Christ. But the line's backing up."

By the way, Mama had a surefire way of handling obscene phone callers. She witnessed to them. The moment she picked up the phone, the guy on the other end didn't have a chance.

"Hello . . . ?" she'd say. "I beg your *pardon?* Young man! Did you know that Jesus Christ suffered, bled, and died on the cross so you could have eternal life? Did you know he was buried in a borrowed tomb and rose again on the third day? Did you know he could set you free from this phone perversion? Get on your knees right now. I

✗Nope, still nothing down here.

16

said, GET ON YOUR KNEES RIGHT NOW and repeat this prayer after me: Say, 'Dear Lord, come into my life, forgive me of my SINS!'. . . Hello?"

Most of them hung up on Mama, but a few of them got saved and became deacons.

Mama even witnessed to Madalyn Murray O'Hair when I was a little kid.

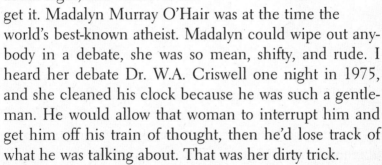

Madalyn Murray O'Hair vs. My Mama.

It happened when I was about eight, and I'll never forget it. Madalyn Murray O'Hair was at the time the world's best-known atheist. Madalyn could wipe out anybody in a debate, she was so mean, shifty, and rude. I heard her debate Dr. W.A. Criswell one night in 1975, and she cleaned his clock because he was such a gentleman. He would allow that woman to interrupt him and get him off his train of thought, then he'd lose track of what he was talking about. That was her dirty trick.

Well, the difference between Mama and Dr. Criswell is that Mama is not a gentleman. You can't interrupt Mama. Mama doesn't have to breathe. Mama can go for days on one breath.

My brother and I were down the hall in our room, listening on the radio to Madalyn running over everyone who called in.

I thought, "Oh, lady, have fun. Mama's on hold."

Finally, the commentator said, "Beverly—" that's Mama. "Beverly, you're on the air."

Have you ever seen the moment at an auto race when the starting guy waves that flag and the cars vroom into action?

That was Mama.

VROOOOM. The flag was down, and Mama was off to the races.

Madalyn kept saying, "Ma'am . . . ma'am . . . ma'am . . . what church do you go to?"

But Mama went vrooming right on. VROOOM, VROOOOOOOOM!

Madalyn kept trying to interrupt: "Ma'am . . . what church do you go—?"

Mama: VROOOOOOOOOM!

"Ma'am, ma'am! What church—?"

Mama: VROOOOOOOOOOOOOOOOOM!

While down the hall my brother and I were yelling: "Get her, Mama!"

Well, Mama gave her the whole Bible. She started in Genesis, and she went straight through to the maps.

Finally, the last thing Mama said was the only thing I remember her saying. But I'll never forget it.

She said, loud and proud, "You asked me how I know he LIVES? He lives within my HEART!"

There was dead silence on the radio for a solid five seconds. Finally, the commentator spoke up, mumbling like he was crawling out from underneath the table.

He said, "Uhm, ma'am, would you please tell her what church you go to?"

When Mama hung up, we heard Madalyn say, "That woman is very intelligent, but she's dangerous."

I thought, *Madalyn, if you only knew.*

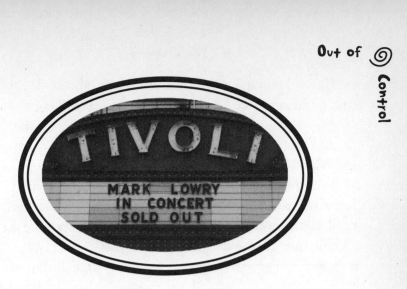

Mama and the Next-Door Neighbor

When I was a kid, our next-door neighbor was Helen Hanft.

That's H-a-n-f-t, Helen Hanftttt.

She had a son named Fritzy. Fritzy Hanftttt.

I used to beat the tar out of him. We'd start out just wrestling, and he would end up runnin' home crying.

I'll never forget Helen. She was short and had the hairiest toes I've ever seen on a woman. She was the only person I knew who could grow her own furry slippers.

She wouldn't go barefoot because she was afraid she'd get split ends.

Helen didn't like me.

I have no idea why.

But when Mama was about thirteen months pregnant with my little sister, Helen walked up to Mama outside

19

our house, pointed at Mother's stomach, and said, "I hope that child isn't like Mark."

Mama swung around like only a pregnant woman can do and said, "Listen here, Helen. One day God is going to use Mark."

When I was a hyperactive kid coming home with notes from my teachers hanging on my lapels, Mama would read those notes, tuck me into my bed, and she'd say, "Mark, one day God's going to use you."

> God believes in us, even when we don't believe in ourselves.

I heard that hundreds of times when I was growing up: "One day, God's going to use you."

I'm thankful for a mother and dad who believed that. Very few people thought that would happen. Especially our next-door neighbor, Mrs. Hanft.

I took Mama to one of my concerts, one with a big SOLD OUT sign on the front. I said, "Did you ever think that would happen?"

She said, "I believed it thirty years ago."

I was lucky to have a mama who believed in me.

Helen Hanfts are everywhere. Bet yours is next door, too. And just in case you don't have a mama like mine, I've got a message for you.

God believes in us, even when we don't believe in ourselves. I know beyond a shadow of a doubt that God has a great plan for everybody's life—yours and mine. And don't you forget it.

God's going to use you.

20

Paw Paw's Chin

I used to think alot about having plastic surgery, because I've got Paw Paw's chin.

Mama's daddy, my Paw Paw, had a big old chin.

He had one of those chins that enters the room three minutes before the rest of him. In fact, it looked like two big chins, because it had a dimple right in the middle of it.

And I got it, too.

It's like a family heirloom, handed down from generation to generation.

Paw Paw had a great, long life. When he died, I went to his funeral—which is always a good time to go. I walked into the back of the funeral home, looked down the aisle toward where Paw Paw lay in his casket, and I couldn't help but laugh. You guessed it. All you could see was his chin sticking up out of that casket.

My chin.

They had to turn him on his side before they could close the lid. (Of course, it was a good place to hang the wreath.)

I know you aren't supposed to laugh at funerals, but since I got his chin I couldn't help it. I'm popular at parties. People rest their cups on it. Why, I think he'd be proud to see how his chin's grown on me.

In fact, I'm so inspired about my hand-me-down chin, I sing a song about it.

(You can hum it to the tune of "Place in This World," if Michael W. Smith doesn't care.)

It goes like this:

Mark Lowry

My hairline's moving, but I am standing still.
A chin like Leno's, nose big as a hill.
A face that's perfect is always in my dreams.
Hope they can fix mine without too many seams.
That's why . . .
I'm looking for a surgeon who'll work overtime to find
My face in this world.
My face in this world.
Not a lot to work with, I need his knife to help me find
My face in this world,
My face in this world.
A million changes, I want Smitty's kind of chin.
All the girls would love my Steven Curtis Chapman
*   grin.*
Give me Carman's eyebrows, but a bit more overgrown.
I'll be a vision, a face almost my own.
That's why . . .
I'm looking for a surgeon who'll work overtime to find
My face in this world,
My face in this world.
Not a lot to work with, but I need his knife to help me
*   find*
My face in this world.
My face in this world. ✘

Bedtime Stories

I'm a college graduate. After I crammed four years of college into five, Mama went to school. She earned a psychology degree.

She carried a 4.0 average all the way through and went on to earn her master's degree. She graduated Summa Cum Laude.

I graduated Thank The Laude. (I know, it's an old joke. And I'll thank you to respect it.)

She's writing a book now about hyperactive children. I gave her the title for it. I said it should be called, *How to Raise a Hyperactive Child and Live to Tell about It.*

I told her, "Mama, there's one good thing about having a hyperactive kid. We frost hair for free."

Mama's hair turned gray, and Daddy's turned loose.

Do you have a hyperactive child? Let me tell you something. Be very careful how you treat that hyperactive kid God gave you, because one day he'll decide what nursing home you go to.

If you're a hyperactive person, you don't need much sleep, especially when you're a kid, because that's a good eight hours you could be partying down in the house when everybody else has wimped out.

My dad, though, had a very special way of getting me to bed. He would tell my brother and me bedtime stories, and we loved Dad's bedtime stories. He didn't find them in magazines; he didn't read them in books. He made them up, right out of his quiet imagination.

Every night, my brother and I lived for bedtime,

because we knew, sure enough, at nine o'clock sharp, Daddy was going to tell us a story. We would run to our bed, and we'd pull the sheets up to our eyes.

(We slept together because I told my brother that one night someone might try to kidnap us. Once, Mama heard me. She said, "Mark, don't worry about it. If they kidnapped you, they'd have you back before morning.")

Every night at nine o'clock, we'd run to our bed and wait, and sure enough, my daddy's hairy arm would reach around the doorpost and turn out the light.

Then in the dark, Daddy and the skull would enter. Dad had bought a skull that glowed in the dark. And that skull would peek around the doorpost and come floating into the darkness. It would float over to our little bed, look down in our little eyes, and Daddy's voice would whisper, "Long ago and f-a-r-r-r-r away, there were two little boys named Mike and Mark . . ."

"That's us!" I'd yell.

And Daddy would tell some scary story that would make the hairs on the back of our necks break dance. It would be a killer of a story.

We were always in them. He didn't read them in books; he didn't get Dick and Jane to be the leading characters. Mike and Mark were the heroes of my dad's stories.

And the scarier the story the better. We didn't want lilacs and springtime. We wanted scary! No matter how scary it got, though, it didn't bother us. We knew at the end we were going to win. Because we knew who was telling the story. We knew that no matter how slimy, how greasy, or how ugly the monster who was chasing us down the corridors of the Oooo-Eeeeee Castle, we knew we were gonna turn on that monster and zap him ugly and stupid by the end of the story.

Because Daddy was telling the story.

And then after the scary story, before we'd fall asleep, Daddy would tell us another story.

He'd tell us about Jesus, and somehow Daddy could put that story on our level. He told us that when Jesus was on this earth, he was a poor man according to the world's standards. He never owned a house. And he never drove a car, which blew my young mind. Of course, I found out later that no one drove cars back then, but to a four-year-old, that fact was quite  impressive. Daddy told us that Jesus was so poor that even when it came time for Jesus to pay his taxes, he had to go fishing to do it. But Jesus, Daddy told us, had something that money couldn't buy, and he was always passing it out.

Daddy said Jesus passed a crippled boy one day. Jesus couldn't afford a wheelchair to give the boy, so he just gave that boy new legs. Another day, Jesus passed a blind kid, and since he couldn't afford a seeing-eye dog, he gave that kid new eyes. Another time, Jesus passed a demon-possessed man, and since he couldn't afford psychiatric counseling, he just cast out the devils and gave that man a sound mind.

And then one very important day, Daddy told us, Jesus passed a little girl's funeral and . . .

This is where it got good.

Every time Daddy told about Jesus and dead people,

we were all ears. Mike and I might fight those slimy, ugly monsters and in our minds slay them ugly, stupid, and dead. We might even get rid of a few demons we found lurking around us, too. But when we heard our daddy tell us about Jesus' biggest power, we were all ears.

Jesus, Daddy would say, was the greatest preacher who ever lived, and he never preached a funeral.

Know why?

"Why?" we'd ask.

Because he raised the dead.

And so the Lord touched the little dead girl's cold, lifeless hand, and—you know the rest—her cheeks flushed pink and healthy. Then she sat straight up. And, folks, when the dead sit up, that funeral is O-V-E-R! Everybody can go home (if they don't drop dead first).

Now that was a bedtime story. The greatest ever told.

And we never got tired of hearing it.

The Greatest Story Ever Told

Mama decided she wanted me to see what I had heard about in Daddy's Bible bedtime stories.

So Mama took Mike and me to see a movie entitled *The Greatest Story Ever Told.*

I had heard the story in Mrs. Gresham's Sunday school class. I had heard the story all my long four-year-old life. And now, through the miracle of Hollywood, we were going to see it.

Mama grabbed me by one hand and Mike by the other hand then led us into the packed theater where the movie was playing. She found three seats beside each other, about halfway in the middle, and we sat down, Mama sitting between us, of course, so we wouldn't fight. I pulled down my seat and crawled up on the edge of my heels so I could get up high enough to see around the adult watermelon-head sitting in front of me.

And that screen, WHEW!

When you're four, a movie screen is BIG. (Everything is bigger and better when you're four. If you don't believe that, go back and look at the house you lived in when you were four and see how much it has shrunk.)

And then, suddenly, up on that BIG screen, there were BIG people walking and talking all over it. They were telling Daddy's and Mrs. Gresham's Bible stories!

And I didn't even have to be in bed or go to church to hear 'em.

My eyes grew big and wide as my whole world filled with the story of Christ. It started with Jesus' birth. Then it went into his childhood. When it came to the part about Jesus wandering away from his mother and teaching at the temple, I thought, "My kind of kid! He ditched his mom!"

Mary, his mother, was out of her mind looking for him. "Where's Jesus?"

Where was he? He was confusing and confounding all the elders, that's where he was. "This kid is all right!" I kept thinking.

And then the movie went into his ministry, starting with Jesus turning water into wine, the first miracle he

27

performed. You gotta love a guy whose first miracle is to keep a party going. And the miracles continued: Jesus gave sight to the blind, speech to the mute, legs to the lame, hearing to the deaf, a new mind to the demon-possessed, then—an eye-popper—fed thousands of people with a little boy's lunch.

> You gotta love a guy whose first miracle is to keep a party going!

But of all the miracles, my favorite story was when he loved the children. He sat down on a rock and let all those little ankle-biters crawl up in his lap.

That's the reason I know Jesus had a good sense of humor. Children won't like you if you look mean and sad all the time. How many kids ever run up to that sourpuss deacon sitting on the back pew of your church? Jesus must have winked and smiled at the children, because they crawled up in his lap. He even let the hyperactive kids get up next to him. I saw them.

I remember thinking, "All right, Jesus!" Because, even by the age of four, few adults wanted hyperactive me in their laps.

That's when one of the bodyguards—which is what I called the disciples—came over and said, "Keep these kids away from Jesus." Jesus stood up and he rebuked that disciple. "Suffer the little children to come unto me, and forbid them not," he told the guy. "For of such is the kingdom of heaven."

And so the movie went. He loved the children, he healed the sick, he raised the dead, he fed the hungry.

Two and one-half hours into the movie, the people

waved and waved and waved palm branches, yelling, "Hosanna! Hosanna! Blessed is He who comes in the name of the Lord!" as Jesus rode through their town on a little donkey. They laid those palm branches down and worshiped him, still yelling, "Hosanna! Hosanna! Hosanna!"

And I remember thinking, "Yeah! Hosanna! Hosanna! He is everything Daddy said he was. Hosanna!"

But then everything changed.

The same people who had been saying, "Hosanna!" were now screaming, "Crucify him!" And that pretty much confused me.

How could those people change their minds so fast?

What were they? Stupid?

Then I found out why. The camera zoomed in on one guy who played the devil. I'll never forget that beard and the wicked look in his eye. Sneaking around in the crowd, he was yelling over and over, "Crucify him!"

And the stupid crowd started yelling it, too.

"Yeah! Crucify him!"

That was bad enough. But then old serpent Satan slimed his way over to the other side of the crowd, and the camera followed him. And now he was saying, "Give us Barabbas!"

And the crowd screamed back like it was their big idea: "Give us Barabbas!"

It got louder and louder and louder. They screamed, "Crucify him, crucify him!"

Crucify him! Crucify him!

Crucify him! Crucify HIM!

CRUCIFY HIM!

And finally, as it got louder and louder, I had all any four-year-old could take. I sat up on the edge of my heels, which were now fast asleep, and, as loud as I could, I screamed:

"NOOOOOOOOOOO!"

My brother leaned over my mother and shouted, "Shut up, Mark, or we'll all go to hell!"

I thought I was going to put a stop to it, and he was scared to death that I might.

But there was no four-year-old boy on that hillside two thousand years ago screaming.

Peter was standing by a fire denying he even knew who Jesus was.

His own mother didn't even try to stop the crucifixion. That has always amazed me. Because she loved him. She loved him probably more than she loved her other children. After all, he was perfect.

He'd be handy around the house, too. Clean the backyard pool? no big deal. He could walk on the water. But can you imagine being his little brother? I can hear Mary now: "Why don't you act like Jesus?"

I'd have answered, "Well, Mom, why don't *you* act like Jesus?"

Think about taking biology class after your big brother Jesus, for instance. "Well, now, Jesus made straight A's."

"Sure, he did. He wrote the book."

But Mary was silent when it came to watching her son die. That's fascinating to me. If I were being crucified in the center of town, my mama would have been pitching a fit.

But Mary didn't open her mouth. I used to wonder why. I'm not sure I know the real answer, but I think it could be that, beyond anyone there, she knew Jesus was virgin-born. If anybody knew who Jesus truly was, she knew it. The baby boy she delivered that first Christmas was now on a cross delivering her.

Mary needed a Savior, too. When we get to heaven and find Mary and the half-brothers of Jesus there, it will be because they, like us, acknowledged that Jesus wasn't just a good prophet, a good preacher, a good teacher, or even a perfect older brother or son.

He was God on foot.

I even wrote a song about it. In fact, I think I'll sing it for you right now:

MARY, DID YOU KNOW?

Mary did you know
*   that your baby boy will one day walk on water?*
Mary did you know
*   that your baby boy will save our sons and daughters?*
Did you know
*   that your baby boy has come to make you new?*
This child that you've delivered will soon deliver you.

Mary did you know
*   that your baby boy will give sight to a blind man?*
Mary did you know
*   that your baby boy will calm a storm with his hand?*
Did you know
*   that your baby boy has walked where angels trod?*
When you kiss your little baby, you've kissed the face of
*   God.*

The blind will see.

31

Mark Lowry

The deaf will hear.
The dead will live again.
The lame will leap.
The dumb will speak the praises of the Lamb.

Mary did you know
*   that your baby boy is Lord of all creation?*
Mary, did you know
*   that your baby boy will one day rule the nations?*
Did you know that your baby boy is heaven's perfect
*   lamb?*
This sleeping child you're holding is the great I Am! **X**

For a four-year-old, the movie version of *The Greatest Story Ever Told* lived up to—and way past—a father's first storytelling version of it.

For an adult—this adult—the original version gets better every time I hear it.

SECOND HALF

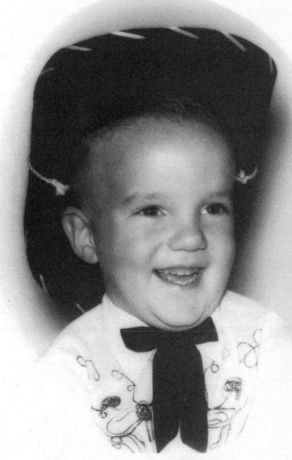

Life as a Brat

The Old Sanctuary

Our shoutin' Baptist church back home in Houston, Texas, didn't have pews. It had individual seats.

It was a fan-shaped church, which I think is kind of cool, because everybody is closer to the preacher. In long, skinny churches, you can be back so far that you spend the whole time squinting.

But our church was like a real auditorium with individual pull-down seats and armrests. Of course, that meant if you're too fat you couldn't come to our church or else you'd be carrying part of it home with you when you left.

Plus those seats would pop you in the rear when you stood up, so you had to be quick.

If you were skinny and quick, you were welcome at our church.

If I ever build a church, I'm not going to have the same kind of seats. I'm putting in La-Z-Boys with Big Gulp holders and a remote control. I figure, if you're going to sleep, you might as well enjoy it.

✗ ⸬♡⸬ ♫

Mama played the piano Sunday morning, Sunday night, Wednesday night, and every special night in between. And as I said earlier, we were always there filling our pew. Every time the church doors were open, the Lowry family was in church.

And our church piano wasn't off in another room or over at the side. No sir. Our piano was slap-dab behind the pulpit.

Mama loved to play that piano, look out at people, and nod and smile.

Sometimes I'd ask her, "Mama, can I go sit up in the shelf?"

Sometimes she'd let me. I'd grab all my friends and we'd go up to the balcony for the service. She'd be playing and singing some song like "Victory in Jesus," and I'd be up in the back row of the balcony learning stand-up comedy for my friends.

When I do concerts, the lights in the auditoriums are usually dimmed, and I have a spotlight shining in my face. I feel like I'm singing to a train. Everyone could be real quiet and sneak out, and I'd never know it.

If there had been spotlights in our church, I'd have gotten a lot less whippings. But I wasn't that lucky. Mama could see me.

Oh, Mama could see me.

Mama was looking out at the crowd with her sweet smile while her fingers caressed "Victory in Jesus" out of those ivories. And I'd be in the balcony cutting up, hoping she wouldn't think to look up to the shelf.

But she did.

Suddenly in the middle of all that good playing, sweet smiling, and nice nodding, she'd spot me in the balcony cutting up and her smile would turn to stone. (I don't know why she got so upset just because I tied my suspenders together and was using them as a bungee cord.) But I tell you what, all she had to do was clear her throat, and I could hear it. Above the singing, I could hear it. And when I looked down, she'd be mouthing words to me.

She knew I could lipread.

While everybody was singing, "O victory in Jesus, my Savior forever," Mama was lip-syncing, "I'm going to WHIP you when we get home."

And if Mama didn't find me, Daddy would. And my church-deacon daddy didn't miss much. His arm could wrap around our church four times, never leave his shoulder, and find the back of my head: POW!

If I were real bad, do you know where he took me?

To the old sanctuary.

Every church ought to have an old sanctuary. Our old sanctuary was haunted.

It had shadows of dead choir members on the walls.

He'd pop me on the back of the head, then lean over to me and say in his God-voice: "COME WITH ME."

"Where're we going?" I'd wail.
"The old sanctuary."
"What FOR????" I'd wail louder.
"CHOIR PRACTICE."

Miss Barth

Somehow I made it to the sixth grade.

The problem was I had a teacher that year who hated my guts. I didn't care for her guts much either. She was my reading and spelling teacher. And the only classes in which I always made straight A's were reading and spelling. So I was bored.

When a hyperactive person gets bored, things pop into his brain he has no control over. Things like, "Get up and run around the room." That, for all you perfect people out there, will get you a spanking.

My sixth-grade teacher had a deal worked out with my daddy. It was called "Two for the Price of One." If I got a spanking in school, I got a spanking at home. So I'd do my best to sit quietly at my desk and not get spankings.

But usually my best wasn't quite good enough.

The reason my teacher didn't like me was because of the way I pronounced her name. She had a wonderful

FLASH! A secret message awaits you between pages 40 and 41 of the 3rd hymnal on the left side of the 7th pew in your church.

38

name. I didn't give her this name, but I had a lot of fun with it. Her name was Miss Barth.

B–A–R–T–H

Just think about what any normal kid could do with that name, much less a hyperactive one.

I'd come into class every day and say, "Well, hello, Miss (and then I'd do my best barfing sounds) BAAARRRTTTHH!"

You know, what's funny to a sixth-grader isn't always funny to an adult.

Miss Barth was a big lady. She had thighs in separate zip codes. She could turn around once and erase a whole blackboard. And her hairdo. I've never seen anything like it before or since. It was HUGE! It looked like ten cow patties with a hairnet over it. I mean, you could house missionaries on furlough in that beehive.

I'd sit there in the back of her class, take out my pad and pen, and do everything possible to keep my hyperactive brain occupied.

Actually, it didn't take much to entertain me. I would make up big words that only I knew what they meant. Then I'd write letters with these words. This might not sound like much, but I would try anything to keep from getting those paddlings.

Miss BAAARRTTTHH found a letter I had written one day with these words I had made up. She came waddling over to me with the letter in her hand. You could hear her coming. Her thighs were apologizing to each other ("'Scuse me, pardon me, 'scuse me, pardon me, 'scuse me, pardon me").

Whenever she'd get upset, she'd shake her head, and that hairdo would flop back and forth. It looked like a demon-possessed poodle. And that day it was flopping around so much I was dodging hairpins.

She stuck that letter right in my face.

"Mark," she said, "what is this?"

I said, "Why I have no idea, Miss Barth. How are you today?"

Okay. That's not what I said at all. That's what I SHOULD have said.

What I said was, "Can't you read?"

"This letter doesn't make any sense," she informed me. As if I didn't know. The nuances of my own personal language were obviously lost on her. So, with those cow patties shifting menacingly there on top of her head, she huffily said, "Why don't you write something that makes sense?"

I said, "Okay, Miss Barth, I will."

So the very next day, I brought her a letter.

It said:

> *Dear Miss Barth.*
>
> *Your feeble attempt to participate in any intelligent conversation only goes to exaggerate your already pathetic lack of mental ability.*
>
> *Sincerely,*
>
> *Mark Lowry*

I got a three-day "vacation."

Mama came to pick me up at school. But that wasn't the worst part. The worst part was when Daddy came home.

Oh, my, Daddy always came home.

As a matter of practice, before spanking me, he'd set me down and explain why I was getting spanked. Because, usually by the time he got to me, I would have forgotten.

But this time, he surprised me. He said something different. My Daddy—did I mention he was a lawyer?—said, "Mark, if you ever, ever write anything like that again, don't sign it!" ✗

Miss Johnson and Mrs. Holland

As I've been saying, I was a hyperactive kid. (Hyper-*creative*—that's what Mama called me, God bless her.)

Attention Deficit Disorder, or ADD, is the fancy name for it. I was on Ritalin for most of my childhood. Every night, Mom and Dad used to tuck me into bed after I had my whipping (Doesn't everybody get a spanking every night before going to bed?), hand me a glass of water, and say, "Mark, one day God's going to use you. But until He does, take this pill."

My teachers didn't have an opinion about whether or not God was going to use me, but they sure enough had one about whether I took that pill.

✗ **Boy**, (boy) n. 1) a noise with dirt on it.

I had a teacher in the third grade named Miss Johnson. I'll never forget her. I was in her class for a whole week. She was so pretty. She had long black hair and long, beautiful fingernails. And they weren't press-ons; these were homegrown.

I knew that for a fact. From personal experience.

Every day I would come home from school with her fingernail prints on my arms.

My mother went down to the principal and said, "I know he's hyperactive, and I know he's a handful. But he's coming home from school with fingernail prints on his arms from his teacher. I want him moved to another teacher's classroom."

So they transferred me to Mrs. Holland's class. Mrs. Holland was older than Miss Johnson and had taught for many years. In fact, she seemed about ten years older than God when I met her.

She had big fluffy hands. And when I would get hyper, she would take me on walks around the Hollybrook Elementary School while the student teacher took over the class. When I couldn't sit still, instead of fussing at me or grabbing me, she'd say, "Mark, let's go for a walk."

She told me the same thing that my parents always told me. She told me that God had a special place for hyperactive kids and that it was okay to be hyperactive. She told me God liked hyperactive kids.

And God liked me.

I had never heard anybody say God *liked* me before. I had heard people say God *loved* me. God has to love you, I mean, he's God, and God is love, and that's what he does. It's his job.

But I had never heard he *liked* me.

There is a difference, you know. There are lots of people I love that I don't really like. Hey, I go through Thanksgiving and Christmas, too.

Oh, don't sit there and act like you don't know what I mean. You know exactly who I'm talking about. You-Know-Who popped into your head. You'll cry at his funeral, but you don't want to go on vacation with him. Yeah, that's who. (And if no one popped into your head—you're probably it.)

But God loves AND likes us.

There are two types of people in the world: Hyperactive and boring. Mrs. Holland told me God loves them both, and God likes them both.

God likes me.

Several years ago, Mrs. Holland's daughter wrote me and said that Mrs. Holland was going to retire from teaching the third grade.

She said, "My mother has talked about you to every third-grade class since you were in her class."

I didn't doubt that. She had written novels about me, too—while I was still in her class, that is. I wore them home from school every day.

Her daughter asked, "Would you write her a congratulatory letter?"

So I sat down and wrote her a letter.

"Dear Mrs. Holland," I wrote, *"The difference between you and Miss Johnson was, Miss Johnson had fingernails that loved flesh, but you had hands that loved children. I want to thank you for loving me and telling me that God liked me."*

Last to Be Picked

I HATE SPORTS.

There, I've said it. And it feels SO good.

Besides the fact I'm about as coordinated as a blob of Silly Putty, I have always hated any kind of activity that made me sweat.

I hate to sweat.

My idea of an exercise program is one sit-up a day. I do half in the morning when I get out of bed and the other half in the evening when I lie down.

My dad still tells about the time that he had me working in the yard and I said, "You want me to go get some iced tea?"

"Okay," he had answered, "go get some iced tea."

He came in later and found me watching TV with a glass of iced tea on the table.

That's pretty much the way I felt about P.E., too. I sure didn't need to get my adrenaline pumping. It was pumping all the time. I had a hard time staying still long enough for a ball to get to me. So I have never understood sports. Okay?

Besides. I hate everything I'm not good at.

If you believe TV, the world revolves around The Home Team, and sneakers cannot be sold without some highly paid sports superstar making commercials for 'em.

Hey, they don't even tell us who the guys are in those commercials anymore, because they figure we know.

I've decided not to follow any particular team or sports figure. I even bought my last pair of sneakers without celebrity help (although the shoe salesmen resembled Elvis). I don't know any sports celebrities' names and have no intention of finding out who they play for, because I don't care. It's hard to care. After all, none of them know who I am. They don't follow my career, so why on earth should I follow theirs?

That's the only thing I hate about Thanksgiving—football, that is.

What a stupid game. A bunch of guys out on a field with a weird-shaped leather ball. Butting heads. Moving a few feet at a time. It takes so long for anything significant to happen. Every now and then, someone will add a little excitement by getting that ball all to themselves and high-tailing it to the right end of the football field.

But I confess. I couldn't care less if Dallas or Denver or Hong Kong won the Super Bowl. If the entire NFL went on a cruise, the ship sank, never to be heard from again, and pro football ceased to exist, my life wouldn't change one iota.

Well, maybe it would change a little bit.

On Thanksgiving, after the big turkey and dressing, green peas, glazed carrots, homemade rolls, sweet-potato casserole, pumpkin AND pecan pie (with whipped cream), it is nice to go to the living room where Dad and Mike are watching football. I lie down, and within thirty seconds, I'm in a coma. I feel no guilt for taking this restful nap because football is on the television. A mindless, worthless, futile, irrelevant-to-the-world football game.

And that's pretty much the value of a professional football game for me—it's a great time to take a Thanksgiving nap.

I really have tried to play different sports. That's why I hate them. They usually ended up playing me.

I am absolutely, totally, without question, the most uncoordinated person I have ever known who is not completely paralyzed or dead. When God was passing out coordination he skipped me. When I was a little kid I went out for peewee baseball. They made me the water boy.

THE WATER BOY.

Can you believe it?

I was the one who brought the OTHER kids their WATER.

Give me a break. You KNOW I looked forward to putting on my little uniform with the double ZERO on the back to lug water to all the other boys.

And it only got worse as I got older.

When I was in elementary school, the teacher would make everyone line up. Two kids were chosen to be team captains, and they would choose up the sides. With the saddest look I could muster, I'd gaze woefully at each captain hoping he'd pick me. But in my heart I knew he wouldn't. Everyone knew I wasn't going to play—I was going to play around. Even the girls got picked before me.

The story was always the same. Nobody would pick me until the teacher said in a disgusted voice, "We can't get started until somebody picks Mark."

The two captains would stare each other down until one would finally kick the dirt and say, "Okay, I'll take him."

I do remember playing football with friends after church one Sunday. Since there wasn't an *Andy Griffith Show* rerun on TV, I figured, "Why not?"

Besides, they actually WANTED me to play.

So there I was at the end of the field about to receive a spectacular pass from my brother, hands out, running like crazy and guess what—

I CAUGHT it.

And a split second later, I was tackled by a 275-pound bruiser.

Parts of me I didn't even know I had were snapping. I sounded like a human Rice Krispy hitting a bowl of milk.

That's the thanks I got for catching the ball.

When I was fourteen I went to camp. I had pimples. I was skinny. I still wasn't athletic. The only sport I thought I could participate in was whittling. By the end of the week, my thumb was in a bandage that the camp nurse had made from a curler. I had whittled off my thumbnail. I was so uncoordinated I couldn't even whittle without losing a part of my body.

But one day at camp, June 5, 1973, Jesus picked me. The Captain of the team didn't ask me to become more athletic. He didn't ask me to improve my life. He didn't ask me to get cleaned up before he would pick me. He just picked me. He saw me just as I was and said, "I pick Mark!"

And no one made him do it!

Do I root for that team? You betcha.

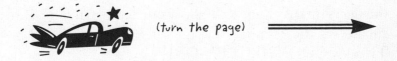

(turn the page)

Daddy and the Slant 6 Plymouth

My parents were true believers in spanking, all right.

I was watching a TV talk show the other day when I heard one of the guests, some pseudo-psychological idiot, say, "Don't ever spank your children. It will squelch their personalities."

I'm here to tell you, Mama squelched my personality all over the house. Until you've been shook so hard that spit flies out of your mouth, swings around, and lands with a slap on the back of your head, you have not had a happy childhood.

And Daddy was such a true believer that he could do it long distance.

You see, I was such a brat that I almost had a whipping in college.

My brother and I went to Liberty University. We chose Liberty because it allowed students to bring guitars, which most of the other church schools didn't.

And it was thirteen hundred miles from home.

I'll never forget the moment Mom and Dad dropped my brother and me off in the parking lot of the Thomas Road Baptist Church (which was on the main campus at the time). My parents turned their big car around and sped back to Houston (I'm sure that was so I wouldn't see them cry at the thought of not having me around the house . . . those tire marks they left were just a slip in the gearshift). As their taillights were getting smaller and smaller in the distance, I remember thinking, "YE-ES. THANK GOD THEY'RE GONE."

No more parents. No more rules. No more homework. I was in college now!

Right.

The first thing the dean told me to do was get a haircut.

Everyone's hair was so short at Liberty that my school yearbook looks like a bowling-ball catalog.

Then there was the dress code and the curfews.

And the rules. Oh yes, the rules: No dancing, no movies, and no "single dates" until you were a senior.

My dormitory also left much to be desired. It was an old downtown hotel. No TV. No phone. No air conditioning. And our beds were metal jobs they'd purchased from an insane asylum. But I was lucky. I only had one roommate.

Unfortunately, he had come with the bed.

Church schools try hard. They try to keep every student safe and sinless and every parent happy. But this one had yet to handle an ADD freshman.

Make that an ADD freshman with a car.

My dad had found a gray 1973 Plymouth Valiant for my brother and me. It was a great car, but U-U-G-G-LY! It had a slant 6 engine. I don't know what that is, except that they run forever.

And we ran it forever.

My brother and I had a group of crazy friends. Like Mick and Rick, for instance. (Boy, were they talented— they could do face contortions better than mine. They're identical twin brothers and were 5'4" each. I told them if their mother's zygote hadn't split, they would have been 10'8".)

One night I had the car to myself. I decided I was going to take about five girls to eat pizza. So we all piled into the Plymouth Valiant and headed toward Sal's Pizza.

Everything was fine until we started home in the old Plymouth. I was cutting up, acting smart to impress those girls, driving crazy. But then I stopped at a red light.

And there, in front of us, was a hippie-looking van with a bumper sticker that said, *If you see the van rocking, start knocking and come on in.*

At least that's what I thought it said.

What I think it really said was, *If you see the van rocking, DON'T start knocking.*

So, since I was young, stupid, and hyperactive even at seventeen, I threw the car into park, jumped out, ran up to the van, and started banging on the back.

I told you I was stupid.

All of a sudden, every door in that van opened up, and eighteen hundred hippies fell out of the thing. I popped my eyeballs back into their sockets, ran back to my car, jumped in, and locked the door.

What I didn't realize was that all the other doors were unlocked. And the girls weren't getting to them fast enough.

Finally, we had all the doors locked in time.

But there we were. Stuck. At a red light. With eighteen hundred long-haired, *pot-smoking-looking-type* hippies circling the Plymouth.

And when they started KICKING the car, I ran that light, red or not.

But breaking the law didn't stop these crazed hippies. That van chased us all over Lynchburg, Virginia. The slant 6 might have run forever, but it sure didn't run fast. You know when a Volkswagen van can keep up with you, you aren't traveling at the speed of sound. "C'mon, car! C'mon!" I kept yelling.

With those hippies right behind, I dropped the girls off in front of the dorm. But it still wasn't over because I had to drive back around to the YWCA parking lot to park my car then walk back to the dorm where the hippies would surely be waiting for me. I parked, inched out of that Plymouth slant 6, and slunk back in the direction of the dorm, keeping to the shadows.

Meanwhile, though, the girls had rushed inside and told all the football players about it. And by the time I got back, the football players were standing outside with base-ball bats, ready to bop some hippie heads.

Being the shy, squeamishingly intelligent person that I am (I hate the sight of blood—specifically my own), I ducked in the side door, ran up to my room, and checked out the scene from my window. I wasn't about to stay down there where anyone could get hurt, especially me. Then—wouldn't you know it—my PERFECT brother TOLD my dad about it.

And my father grounded me, LONG DISTANCE, from using the car.

He said, "Mark, you can't use the car for a week. If I hear about you using the car, I'll fly up there and I'll whip you. Do you understand?"

I was in college and my father was still threatening to spank me.

Silly, right? Hey, what big-stuff college freshman would have listened to that?

Me, that's who.

It didn't cross my mind to drive the car, because my PERFECT brother would tell him and I'd get a whipping right there in front of the dorm. He'd fly out there and spank me. And I would have had to bend over and let him do it. Talk about rocking and knocking.

Now THAT would have been embarrassing.

My First Most-Embarrassing Moment

"Hey, Mark! What's your most embarrassing moment?"

That's what an interviewer asked me the other day.

Sadly, I didn't have to strain at all to answer.

In fact, I don't just have one big embarrassing moment. Two immediately popped into my head.

My Second Most-Embarrassing Moment happened with the Bill Gaither Vocal Band on stage with thousands of people watching. (I'll tell you that one later. Delayed gratification—make that mortification—is a good thing.)

My First Most-Embarrassing Moment happened when I was fifteen years old. At church camp, I had made friends with a girl who was one of the most fun people I'd ever met. She had a great personality.

And she was blind.

I'd never known a blind person. I just knew they always seemed to dress themselves better than I did. Plus I was fascinated with her watch. It had a crystal that popped up so she could feel the hands and tell the time. I had to try it. It felt cool.

When I asked her if she knew what color her eyes were, she said, "Yes, I picked them out." I thought that was cool, too. We became good friends by the end of that week.

On the last night of camp I had the honor of leading my new friend to the stage to sing a song. The tabernacle where we had our services was an old converted chicken coop. It had no walls, and there were lots of poles holding up the weatherworn tin roof.

I was so excited that my new friend had been asked to sing that as I led her to the front, I led her—you guessed it—right into a pole.

BAMMMM!

The sound of the collision echoed throughout the entire tin chicken coop.

In unison, all five hundred kids in attendance moaned, "Oh, Mark."

They probably thought I did it on purpose. But I didn't. I wanted to die.

When this gracious girl got to the microphone, she just said, "Well, Mark doesn't get his seeing-eye-dog license this year."

Everybody laughed.

Except me. I was sitting behind her wishing the earth would open up and swallow me, even if it had to take two swallows!

And as I watched her sing "He Touched Me," a big knot, with my name on it, grew big, bright, and black and blue on her forehead.

Adventures at Church Camp

In the summer of 1973, like every other summer, I went to church camp.

In fact, that year I was even leading the singing at the camp.

"Beulah Land"—that was its name—was outside of Nacogdoches, Texas, and our church owned it.

Beulah Land was a "running camp."

That's because my church was a "running" church.

We had changed churches by then, from one Baptist church to another, that is. My daddy didn't like the way our old church was teaching that we'd have to go through the Tribulation, because he didn't want to go through the Tribulation. So we moved.

The choice had come down to two churches, and the winner was the one that shouted the most. My dad was tired of a dead church. He wanted a shouting church, even though he never shouts. He wanted one that had some life to it, and he got it. Our new church was a shouting, and sometimes a running, Baptist church. When I say shouting, I'm not talking about speaking in tongues. Their shouting was in English. And their running, well, I don't know what that was. But they'd shout, and when they got excited, they would just take off running.

Sometimes I took off running just to get out of the service.

That worked especially well at church camp. That's why I called it a running camp. You get that many kids together and tell them it's okay to run around during a church service, you're going to see some running, all right.

Of course, it was still your basic church camp in the things that really mattered. Powdered eggs. Separate swimming hours for boys and girls. Ugly leather crafts.

And pranks.

There are traditions to uphold at church camps.

Even running, shouting, Beulah Land Baptist church camps.

One of my best time-honored pranks dealt with glass-vial stink bombs. (Helpful hint: Quality stink bombs are available at novelty shops and magic stores everywhere. I always carry a spare; you never know when you might need a good stink bomb.)

A bunch of guys and I would wake up in the middle of the night and go over to the girls' dorms. All the girls' dorms had window air conditioners. What the girls didn't know was that because of the way the units fit into the window, there was just enough room in the bottom left corner to poke a pair of pliers—holding a stink bomb.

The best part was that, before the bomb had done its work, we could be back in bed watching the lights in the girls' dorm flip on and the girls in their nightgowns rush outside.

And, invariably, you could always hear someone say, "Was that MARK LOWRY?!"

I got blamed for everything (or credited, however you want to look at it).

But during all the prank-pulling, running, shouting, and song-leading, I got saved.

We had two services that night. We had two services every night. My brother got saved in the first service, and I got saved between the two services.

(I had whittled off my thumbnail that week, too, as I've mentioned. I was whittling, turned my thumb the wrong way, and PHEWT! I whittled that thumbnail right off. The camp nurse put a curler on it. I remember the first song I sang after I got saved was, "The Lighthouse." I "thank God for the lighthouse," and I raised that curler to heaven.)

I was talking to Debbie, this deaf friend of mine, after the first service. She was reading my lips by the light of the lamppost.

After I told her how I didn't think I was saved, she said, "Let's pray."

Well, she started praying first. And she kept right on praying. And kept on praying. Since she's deaf, and she had her eyes closed, I thought, "I can't pray until she shuts up. The Lord could come before she quits praying and I'm gonna be left."

Finally she stopped, and I got right with God.

There was a slight problem, though. I was already supposed to be saved. I had joined the church years before. I was the leader in my youth group, for crying out loud. So I thought people would laugh at me since everyone took for granted I was already saved. But they didn't; they were happy.

I've gotten saved many times since then, to tell you the truth. J.D. Sumner says something pretty smart: "God saves me every day."

When you think about it, we *are* being saved every day of our lives. I don't believe you can be born again and again and again, but, boy, it seems like you can.

A good title for life would be: *How to Become a Christian Now That You're Born Again.*

Know what I mean?

But it was real at church camp that night, and things have been different ever since.

Almost everything. While everyone was happy for my spiritual encounter, it sure didn't keep them from blaming me when things kept happening around the camp.

For some reason, when the girls in their nightgowns kept running out of their dorms in the middle of the night, swatting at the stinky air, we still heard, "Was that MARK LOWRY!?"

(Well, God saves you, he doesn't ruin you.)

THIRD HALF

Life on the Road

Pivot on Your Good Foot

When I was in college, I was part of an evangelistic team.

I was not the team comedian.

(Now there's a concept: "Thank you for that inspired rendition of 'Amazing Grace,' and now a few witty sidesplitters to warm you up for the preacher's message! Take it, Brother Lowry!")

I was the singer. Another guy was the preacher, another was the piano player, and another was the driver.

That's right, the driver. Any college evangelical team roaming the country- side every weekend needed a driver. Our preacher guy would lay out a map and put a yardstick to it. If a town landed inside that straight line, he was convinced we could drive it in a weekend and get back for classes Monday morning without breaking land-speed records. So the driver position was an important position. And like Greyhound, we left the driving to him. ALL of it. Hey, the driver drove. The preacher preached, the singer sang, and the piano player, well, he had to rest those fingers. So we couldn't relieve the driver. Uh-uh. We were supposed to sleep. That was our job. And his was to D-R-I-V-E that van A-L-L over creation.

When we first got started, a man in Michigan offered to customize the van to fit our traveling needs.

"What do you guys want?" he asked.

Well, we huddled and came up with the single-most important ingredient for weekend life on the road.

"We want a bed in the back," we agreed. "A big bed. A bed big enough for three guys to sleep WITHOUT touching each other."

We all agreed the last part was very important.

So he customized that van with a big bed in the back and a place to store all our sound equipment and stuff under it.

And we hit the road.

One weekend in March we were booked all the way up in New York. So on Thursday, March 17, we left at midnight.

Jockeying for position was an essential talent when it came to sleeping in a bed with three guys on the road. Jockeying and timing.

See, you don't want to sleep in the middle. We're talking guys—sweathogs. And nobody after a few close encounters of the three-guy-kind wanted to sleep in the middle. If you got stuck like a tuna in a sandwich, you had dragon breath on one side and body odor on the other.

I'd figured out a way to be sure I wasn't the tuna. My secret was this: Get there early, pick a side, crawl into my sleeping bag, and start sawing giant redwood logs. And by the time our driver, Dick, had us rolling, the middle dilemma was a done deal.

And that's what happened that night.

Dave the piano player was in the middle, Charles the preacher was on the other side, and me, I was happily snoring away on my side as we drove through the night toward New York.

By 5:30 in the morning, we had made it to Carlisle, Pennsylvania.

That's right. Dick the driver had been driving five and one-half hours straight—through the dead of night.

Yes. Charles, Dave, and I were asleep in the back.

And Dick was asleep at the wheel.

When you've got your head lying on the dashboard, you've pretty much lost the fight with the sandman.

Well, that van was sliding all over the interstate. We hit the median, we hit the guardrail, and my sleeping bag was rolling ITSELF up by the time my brain got the message from the rest of my body that something dangerous was happening and I ought to come back to full consciousness to check it out.

When I did, I woke up screaming: "WAKE UP, DICK!"

Dick jerked. Which meant the van jerked.

We went spinning around and around and around, bopping the median then the guardrail then the median again, all the way up a hill and down the other side.

"WHOA!" I was thinking, "I should have let the man SLEEP!"

Finally, we screeched and shimmied to a landing at the bottom of the hill—broadside across the two lanes of the highway.

In one piece.

"Thank God this is over," I remember gasping.

But at that exact moment, an eighteen-wheeler topped the hill going seventy miles an hour and came roaring down to play tag with our van.

When an eighteen-wheeler plays tag with your van, you're going to be it.

Next thing I knew there was the biggest, ugliest woman

I ever saw in my life towering over me, staring into my face. That lady flossed with rope! I mean that woman was big, 8'3" if she was a speck.

My soul, how did THAT get in our van? I was thinking.

And then she leaned closer. It looked very much like she was about to perform mouth-to-mouth rescuscitation on me, and I wanted her to know that was not necessary.

"UghGGPHGGH," I grunted out. Translation: I'm awake and breathing F-I-N-E.

"You're in the emergency room," she begged to differ. "How do you feel?"

"I need a chiropractor," I told her.

"You don't need a chiropractor," she begged to differ again.

"Then I need my mama," I said. "My mama'll get me a chiropractor."

And I fainted.

When I woke up, I felt something funny going on with my left leg. I looked up. A doctor was messing with it.

"What are you doing?" I squeaked out.

"We're setting your leg."

As I was passing out again, I remember thinking, "Well, whaddya know. I finally got a broken leg." I always wanted one. One of my childhood desires was to have a broken leg. My brother broke an arm or a leg just about every summer, and the girls would sign his cast, which I thought was cool.

When I woke up again, the doctor said, "You've got ten broken bones."

"Ha!" I thought. "When the kid does it, he does it right."

Then the doctor proceeded to give me a rundown. He started ticking them off: My right pelvis was broken. All my ribs on my right side were broken. My collarbone was broken. And I broke two bones just in my left leg. They didn't need an x-ray to figure out the leg. When you've got two knees on one leg, that sucker is broken.

Add 'em up and whaddya got?

TEN bones.

The morning after the crash I got what's called "fatty embolisms," which has nothing to do with good ol' greasy burgers and fries, let me tell you. When you break lots of bones, fat drops in your blood system and forms clots, which unfortunately cuts off the oxygen supply to your brain, and you go out of your mind. Which in my case was very hard to detect. The doctor actually told my mother I was so bad I'd die within forty-five days or be mentally retarded. ("Okay, Mrs. Lowry! The choices are, die within forty-five days, be mentally retarded, or be out of his mind. The winner is . . .") Well, I didn't die. But you can imagine the eyes on me when I woke up the next day and uttered my first words. And my second. And my third and—you get the picture.

After three days, though, they'd had enough of my laziness. It was time for physical therapy!

I'd never been in physical therapy. It sounded kind of fun. I thought maybe all of us "inmates" got together and played games of Monopoly or exercised our hands with rubber balls in synchronized routines, finishing off with cookies and punch. Yes sir, I thought, "Physical therapy! We're going to have fun."

A candystriper came into my room pushing a wheel-chair. She was cute as a bug, blonde hair, my age—nineteen—blue eyes, and a Pepsodent smile that lit up the room like it came with batteries. This girl would make a bulldog break his chain, she was so cute.

"Hi, Mark! Today I'm gonna take you to physical therapy!" she bubbled.

"Well, let's go!" Never mind the cast down one side of my body and up the other, I slid in that chair as agile and cool as you please. Or so I had it pictured. Truth was I looked more like a white plaster cannon coming down the hall, my left leg's cast was so big and straight. But I didn't have a clue. We were having a great time, that girl and I, chatting away, and all the while I'm thinking she's my physical therapist and, boy, are we going to have fun.

But then she wheeled me into a colorful room and disappeared. And Guess Who was waiting for me. That's right. The nurse who flossed with rope. She wasn't so much ugly as mean. And I found out which was worse. She didn't even introduce herself, but I knew her name.

Her name was Attila the Hun in Orthopedic Pumps.

She marched over to me and announced, "Today I'm going to teach you how to stand up."

Big deal, I thought. I've done that before.

But I'd never done it after breaking ten bones in my body.

I stood up, and all the blood in my body sat back down. Every little white and red corpuscle looked at each other and said, "Hey, let's all go to his left foot. One-two-three-wheeee!"

The blood kept draining right into my foot until my toes looked like little overdone Jimmy Dean sausages.

"Ma'a-A-M!" I howled. "I gotta sit D-O-W-N!"

"Well, then," she snapped, "sit down."

That was it for the first day.

When that cute candystriper came rolling that wheelchair into my room the next day, it wasn't quite the same. She wheeled me into that colorful room and disappeared all over again. And Attila was waiting for me.

She walked over in those orthopedic pumps and repeated, word for word, like she'd punched the same tape from the day before: "Today, I'm going to teach you how to walk."

Oh, my soul, I thought. "I'm probably gonna have to stand up to do that, ain't I?" I asked.

She whipped around to the back of the wheelchair and wheeled me straight over to the parallel bars. The kind those tiny, limber people win Olympic medals twirling and whirling all over.

Somehow I got myself up holding those bars, and when I looked back at Attila, I knew that she was not going to let me go back to my room until I walked.

So somehow I made it to the end of those bars. And when I got down there, she said, "Pivot-on-your-good-foot-and-walk-back-to-me!"

"But—" I stuttered.

"Pivot-on-your-good-foot-and-walk-back-to-me! Pivot-on-your-good-foot-and-walk-back-to-me!" she kept repeating.

"But—"

"Pivot-on-your-good-foot-and-walk-back-to-me! Pivot-on-your-good-foot-and-walk-back-to-me! Pivot . . ."

So I put all my weight on my "good foot." And I got right off it—quick.

"Ooh, OOOOH, ma'a-M!! My good foot sure does hurt," I moaned.

She looked at me, real persnickety, face all pruned-up, and said, "We've x-rayed you from head to toe. Everything that's been broken has been taken care of. So pivot-on-your-good-foot-and-walk-back-to-me!"

We've-x-rayed-you-from-head-to-toe. Everything-that's-been-broken-has-been-taken-care-of, so-PIVOT-ON-YOUR-GOOD-FOOT-AND-WALK-BACK-TO-ME!

So I pivoted. And somehow I managed to make it to the end of those bars. And guess what she said?

"Pivot-on-your-good-foot-and-walk-back-to-me! Again."

"Ma'am, oh Ma' a-aM!" I begged. "My good foot's got to be at least sprained."

"I told you—" she said, the persnickety turned up an extra notch, "We've-x-rayed-you-from-head-to-toe. Everything-that's-been-broken-has-been-taken-care-of, SO-PIVOT-

ON-YOUR-GOOD-FOOT-AND-WALK-BACK-TO-ME!"

Hey! I thought, looking around desperately. Where is everybody else, huh? Where's that Monopoly board, those little rubber balls? Those cookies? HELP me, somebody!

But it was just me, Attila the Nurse, and this one old lady on a stretcher. You know what her physical therapy was? They tilted her up a little bit each day. That was it! That's all they did to her! And during the entire time—the three whole days I was there—this is what I heard coming from her stretcher: "Oh Lord, take me home. Oh Lord, take me home. Oh Lord, take me home. Oh, Lord take me home." After hearing that for three days I started praying, "Oh Lord, take her home."

I knew she'd be a lot better off at home.

After two days of pivoting on my good foot, I figured I'd faint dead away if I had to do it anymore. I begged not to go, and I could beg, I tell ya. But I went. And on the third day of physical therapy, Attila handed me some crutches.

"Today," she announced, "I'm going to teach you how to climb steps."

"Oh, joy of all joys," I thought.

She wheeled me over to these three little steps, stuck one of the crutches under my left arm, stuck the other under my broken collarbone, popping my broken ribs and passing my broken pelvis, landing up next to my "good foot," and said: "Now climb to the top of those steps."

I dragged that cast up to the top of those steps and when I finally got to the top, guess what she said?

"Pivot-on-your-good-foot-and-walk-back-to-me."

"Ma'am!" I said, "I don't OWN a good foot. You got one I can borrow, then I'll pivot!"

By this time, I could say it with her:

"We've-x-rayed-you-from-head-to-toe. Everything-that's-been-broken-has-been-taken-care-of, SO-PIVOT-ON-YOUR-GOOD-FOOT-AND-WALK-BACK-TO-ME!"

✗ ⚡♡⚡ 🎵

The next day, my parents flew me home to Houston, and it took four first-class seats to get me there. I was sprawled out across every one of them. Which meant I got four first-class meals. I ate 'em all and asked for more. I'd been eating hospital food, and when you've been eating hospital food, Sugar, you don't brush your teeth afterwards, you count 'em.

Back in Houston, Daddy took me to the best bone specialist in town. I was awake for the x-ray session this time, wide awake. The kind of awake you get when someone pops a piece of ice down your back. Medical science is a wonderful thing, but they haven't yet learned how to warm an x-ray table. They put me in that backless gown where the wind blows free (you may break every bone in your body, but you better have one good hand left to keep that gown together or you're gonna be showing the world something it doesn't care to see). Then they wheeled me into the x-ray room and plopped me down on the cold steel table. I told the nurse, "It's so cold in this room, you could hang meat in here."

She said, "I know and you're it."

They put me in positions I didn't know I could get into. And I'll never forget what happened next. The doctor, the best bone specialist in Houston, came in, x-rays in hand, and he was clicking like a clock, tsk-tsking all the way to where I waited.

"Tsk-tsk-tsk-tsk-tsk-tsk, Mark, mark Markmarkmarkmark."

"Markmarkmark—"

"WHAT?" I finally yelped.

"Mark, your right ankle is also broken. Their x-rays missed it. I have to put it in a cast, and you can't put any weight on it for three months or I'll have to operate."

Make that ELEVEN bones.

You know that little knob on your foot? My ankle—on my GOOD FOOT—above that little knob was broken clear through.

And the only thing going through my mind was that old heifer saying, *"We've-x-rayed-you-from-head-to-toe. Everything-that's-been-broken-has-been-taken-care-of SO—pivot-on-your-good-foot-and-walk-back-to-me!"*

✗ ☼♡☼ ♫

Life can change in a snap. (And I'm here to tell you every bone in your body can snap in a snap, too.) We were all a mess, but we all survived, even Dick the driver. Charles the preacher was in a coma for a while, and Dave, the one in the middle, was beaten up pretty badly, but didn't break a thing. (There's a moral in there somewhere.) But nothing would ever be the same for us.

Why do you think God let that wreck happen? People were always asking me that. I've thought about that a lot. I started asking the question lying in my hospital bed. I said, "Lord, we've got ninety youth rallies booked for this summer. Now our preacher is in a coma! What are we gonna do? Prop him up and play a tape?"

But after several years of pondering, I finally figured out why God let it happen.

We had the wreck because our driver fell asleep.

That's why. We broke a simple physical law set up by God himself. You fall asleep at the wheel, you got problems. And mere mortals don't ever break God's laws; God's laws break them. If Billy Graham jumped out of the Empire State Building, Billy Graham is still going to splat when he hits the pavement.

And I know something else now, too. Do you know why the driver fell asleep? Because he was driving a bunch of prima donnas around, that's why. No one wanted to relieve the driver. Hey, if we helped out one night, he might expect it every night, and excuse me, my job was to SING. Forget that common sense alone would have gotten one of us up there to give the guy a rest for safety's sake.

We had our pride.

Prima donnas on the road for the Lord . . . the Lord who was himself a servant. He washed disciples' dirty feet. He could have spoken the word, and Peter would've had a pedicure. But he was showing us how to serve each other.

So, why *did* God let it happen? Because *we* let it happen.

Stepping Out on Eleven Broken Bones

One day, when my bones were healing but the casts were still on, Daddy decided I needed to get out.

When we got to the car, he said, "Want to drive?"

Daddy wasn't one to have crazy ideas, so when he did, I wasn't going to stifle the urge. That's how they learn best, you know.

So I drove.

I had one cast on my right leg from ankle to knee, another on my left leg from ankle to hip, and there I was driving around Houston. I had to put my left hand on the door, my right hand on the back of the car seat, and pull myself up to angle my casts in, up, and under the steering column.

When my mother saw us, she about gave birth to triplets.

But then everyone got into the act. I was the best show in town.

I got no respect.

One day, for instance, my friends Kathy, Suzette, Frances, and Jan decided they should take me out to eat.

They were just trying to get back at me, I decided later.

I think it had something to do with the time I took Suzette to the airport, and just before she boarded, fell on my knees, grabbed her around the ankles, and begged her not to leave me and the kids.

She tried walking away and I kept holding on. The more she walked, the louder I got. "Don't leave us, SWEETHEART!" I sobbed. "If not for ME, think of the CHILDREN!"

And here she and her buddies were, packing me off for a big meal in public. If I'd have had half a brain, I'd have been suspicious. Those guys didn't ever stifle a crazy idea.

They packed me into the front, shoved my wheelchair in the trunk, and off we went. When we got to the restaurant, they pulled the wheelchair from the trunk and wheeled it around to my side of the backseat. They had already called ahead and told the restaurant that they had a handicapped person coming, because this was before handicap-access type things were available. So, all was ready.

Except me.

I couldn't get out of the car. I was wedged in. Everybody was helping me, and nothing was working. My rear end got stuck between the curb and the car while my leg was sticking straight up and lodged on the car's roof. Someone outside was pulling on me, someone inside was pushing on me, and I was screaming, "JUST LET ME DO IT! JUST LET ME DO IT!"

By this time a crowd had gathered. And Suzette was about to wet her pants because she was laughing so hard. She had to sit down on the curb.

Finally, we had to get a couple of waiters to help. Those guys got me out, all right. They work hard for those tips.

Finally, the gang wheeled me through the kitchen, which was the only way to get me to our table. And then, just as we made it to the table, just as everybody settled back into their chairs, I realized I had to go to the bathroom.

Groaning, Jan handed me the table's vase. "Just use this."

But when nature calls, nature calls.

So Jan rolled me to the male facilities, where she had to stop, because she was a girl.

Jan waited and waited and waited.

Finally, Jan said a man came out shaking his head and laughing. "There's a clown in that bathroom trying to relieve himself."

No respect, I tell ya.

The Podium with a Lid on It

When I started traveling on my own, the first church I sang in was a Presbyterian church.

I'll never forget how nervous I was. I noticed right off the bat that Presbyterians are richer than Baptists. They must be, I thought. They had two pulpits.

They had one over to the left and one to the right and I thought they must have dueling preaching on Sunday morning or something.

I noticed this as I was sitting on the front row, scared out of my mind, praying (I can do several things at once, one of the blessings of being hyperactive).

"Please don't let me say anything stupid, Lord," I was praying. "Just this once. God, Baptists don't mind, because I'm one of them. But, Lord, I ask you just this once, don't let me say anything stupid."

Then in the middle of praying it again ("Oh, God, don't let me say anything stupid. Please, I'm asking you.

I'll go to Africa, I'll do anything you want me to do, just keep me from saying anything . . ."), I also noticed that they had a podium with a lid on it.

Well, I had never seen such a thing before, and so I thought, in the middle of my praying, "Well, that's pretty. I wonder what that is."

The preacher introduced me, and God did not answer my prayer.

The minute the preacher finished, I walked over and pulled the lid off that podium. It had water in it.

I had yet to say a word or sing a song.

And the first thing I said was, "What is this?"

"That's our baptistry," someone answered.

I looked at the water, then back at the crowd. And I said, "How do you get in there?"

Fortunately, they knew I was a dumb Baptist. Dunked so long, the boy's brain was waterlogged, no doubt.

But it didn't matter.

Baptists, Presbyterians, Methodists, Lutheran, or any of the other thirty-one flavors, it doesn't matter if you've been sprinkled or you've been dunked, if you don't know Jesus you just got wet. **X**

X Guinness Book of World Records—record held by Marla Lou Bass, age thirteen, of Tennehaw, Texas, for longest time held under at a baptism—four minutes and fifty-nine seconds.

Sure Beats Hell

When God called me into the music ministry, I was more surprised than anyone, because to this very day I still can't read music. Sheet music has always looked like a bunch of little white and black boys jumping over a fence.

I said, well, I guess I could sing.

Next thing I know I'm part of an evangelistic team.

Next thing I know after that is my evangelistic team got crunched by an eighteen-wheeler.

After the wreck, I thought it was over.

But then a friend decided he'd be my booking agent. This was a guy who could book a pork chop into a synagogue.

Next thing I knew I was booked for forty-three concerts in forty-one days.

And sometimes my early audiences were not exactly friendly.

So I started talking to fill up the time between songs. And I don't mean "talking," like lots of gospel singers do.

You know what I mean: "This next song is Amazing Grace How Sweet the Sound That Saved a Wretch Like Me, I Once Was Lost and Now Am Found, Was Blind But Now I See," and then they sing it. I'd always think, "Sing it or quote it. We don't have to hear it twice!"

Instead, I began telling them all about Mama. And Mrs. Johnson. And Attila the Nurse. Then I'd sing. Everybody seemed to like it. So I kept on doing it.

It took me a little while to get it right. And the first few times I tried it, well, I don't think I was a rousing success.

I'll never forget the first night.

My first try at going solo was Pittsburgh.

I stood up there in front of the church's congregation and sang and talked and sweated. I did the best I could. I mean, I sang every little song I knew and talked a little bit. When I got through, the preacher walked up, stuck out his hand, and said, "Thank you for coming."

And then he gave me a big old preacher smile.

I gave it right back to him and said, "Thank you for having me."

Then much to my surprise, he just walked away.

That was it.

They didn't take a love offering for me. I didn't have any tapes to sell. I didn't have any T-shirts to sell. I didn't have any videos or black-and-white glossies to sell. I didn't have a thing.

They didn't even give me any gas money or change for McDonald's, and I was hungry.

I was ticked!

I wasn't mad at them. I was mad at God. Have you ever been mad at God? I found something out. When you're mad at God, you might as well go ahead and tell him, because he already knows. And if you don't tell him, you're lying, and you'll have to confess that later. So you might as well spill it.

Which is what I did.

I was driving down that bumpy Pennsylvania Turnpike dodging potholes as big as my little car, and I said, "Lord, your employee didn't get paid tonight. We're going to go broke at this rate! Michael Jackson doesn't even sing for you and he's almost got as much money as you do. God, my stomach likes food, and this car likes gas. We're going to be hitching rides in a matter of days. What are we going to do?"

And the Lord didn't say a word. The Lord never speaks to me audibly. I'm a Baptist; I couldn't handle it.

> The Lord never speaks to me audibly. I'm a Baptist, I couldn't handle it!

The Lord spoke to my heart instead. He said, "Mark, old buddy (he still speaks to me in Texan), whatever they paid you, it's more than you deserved."

That part took care of the self-inflated idea of who I thought I was.

But the Lord just had to go on talking. And the next thing he said to my heart was something I wasn't ever going to forget.

He said, "Hey, Mark, anything above burning in hell is a privilege."

Well.

That was a conversation stopper. I thought about that for a while. So what if I ran out of money before the end of the month—or the end of a Pennsylvania highway? I didn't deserve to stand and sing his praises, much less know his goodness. Because of the Lord's mercy, I wasn't going to spend eternity apart from the love of God, finding out the true definition of "hot." I'm going to live forever.

"Lord," I said, "your employee didn't get paid tonight, but it sure beats hell!"

You know what? That pretty much works on everything. No matter what you go through, compare it to hell, and, boy, can you smile.

Bill Gaither's Bugle

 I travel part-time with Bill Gaither, who is a legend in contemporary Christian music. You know the guy. He's in the hymnal. He's written songs like, "The King Is Coming," and "Because He Lives," and "He Touched Me."

Yeah, THAT Bill Gaither.

In 1988, out of the blue, he called me on the phone. I didn't know him personally. I don't even know how he got my number.

But I knew Bill Gaither discovered Sandi Patty. He was famous for discovering people.

Bill Gaither discovered Larnelle Harris.

Bill Gaither discovered Carman.

Bill Gaither discovered Steve Green.

Bill even discovered George Beverly Shea.

(Okay, maybe not George Beverly Shea. But he could have.)

The list goes on and on. You know what Bill Gaither does best? He discovers your hidden talents. When he found Sandi Patty, she was a bass. Bill said, "You know, if you hit a few high notes, you might really go somewhere."

And when he found Larnelle Harris, he was white.

When Bill found me, I was hyperactive.

But even Bill can't change everybody.

He asked me if I'd like to audition for the Gaither Vocal Band.

I said, "Does Billy Graham have a quiet time? You bet your sweet bippy."

I didn't mention that I can't read music. I didn't think that was the time to bring that up. And I didn't tell him that I had never sung baritone before. I didn't want to bring that up, either.

I auditioned, and not too much later, he asked me if I'd like to join the group. And singing with Bill and the Vocal Band have been the most exciting years of my life.

When I first joined the group, I thought he must be perfect to have written such great songs.

He's got a big fancy bus. And he owns it because he wrote "He Touched Me."

I wrote "Big Booger Blues," but that won't get you a bus. (Okay, I didn't really write "Big Booger Blues," but I could have.)

He's also a bonafide genius because he married Gloria. What would he be without her? A bunch of music with no words, that's what. (They are so in love, too. One night before a concert, I saw Gloria running her fingers through his hair. It was a wonderful romantic moment, until Bill came in and demanded it back.)

In the back of Bill's fancy bus, he's got a bedroom where he and Gloria sleep. While the rest of us are in bunks piled on top of each other, they've got a bedroom. They've got two beds back there, kind of a Ricky-and-Lucy thing going on, but you didn't hear that from me.

On my first trip traveling with them, I'd catch myself sometimes just staring at him, thinking, "I'm traveling with somebody who's in the hymnal right along with Fanny Crosby." And to travel with somebody in the hymnal is incredible because Fanny doesn't get out much these days.

Then, during one of those first trips, Bill said I could sleep back there in the other bed because Gloria wasn't going with us. So I was in one bed, and he was in the other bed. (That's the way we like it, you know.) I had gone to bed first. I woke up about two in the morning and looked over in Bill's bed. I thought he wasn't there, because all I saw was a pile of pillows. Come to find out, Bill Gaither, Mr. He Touched Me, sleeps under pillows. He doesn't sleep under blankets like a normal person. He roots like a dog under a pile of pillows.

I knew he was under there, because I saw his nose peeking through those pillows. Actually, it wasn't peeking; it was standing out boldly, proudly. And I started staring at his nose, thinking, "That is Bill Gaither's nose."

Then he moved around a little, getting comfortable. And I saw his hands and his face pop out.

"There's perfect Bill Gaither's perfect hands that wrote those greats songs," I thought sleepily.

And there was perfect Bill Gaither's perfect lips, the first to ever to speak those legendary lyrics. "There's just something about that name," I added to myself wistfully.

And there was perfect Bill Gaither's perfect nose that's been forming his high notes for over forty years now, I continued on with my dreamy train of thought.

And while I was chugging along with my perfect thoughts, staring at Bill Gaither's perfect nose—

—that nose let me down.

It started snoring. First it was perfect little snorts, nothing to tarnish his image or anything. It was sort of like a pig digging for roots. Then it went on to become the sound of a freight train hitting a bridge at about ninety miles an hour.

And it didn't stop there. It went on to the sound of a 747 nosediving to find a seat at the Crystal Cathedral from thirty-thousand feet.

Then his head started spinning around and around and spewing green stuff all over the . . .

(Just kidding.)

Actually, I wouldn't even have minded all the noises Bill Gaither's perfect nose was making, as long as he'd kept a rhythm going.

But it didn't stop there. And it didn't stop all night.

After that first time traveling on the Gaither bus, and after all the years since—exciting as they have been— all I've got to say is that Bill Gaither may have written "The King Is Coming," but folks, when the King does come, you'd better pray Bill isn't asleep.

Because we'll never hear Gabriel blowing his horn if Bill's blowing his.

My Second Most-Embarrassing Moment

My First Most-Embarrassing Moment that I've already confessed in detail was back in church camp during my years as a church brat. (Don't remind me.)

My Second Most-Embarrassing Moment happened a few years ago when I was singing at the Gaithers' Annual Familyfest in Gatlinburg.

Bill had me do one of my monologues. I was making the usual ugly faces that go with the routine when I heard someone from the audience yell, "Your face is gonna stick like that!"

I tried to ignore him. I'm not used to being heckled, especially by Gaither's crowd. I mean, let's face it. Gaither does draw an older audience. They don't throw tomatoes; they throw bran muffins.

So I just continued with my monologue, hoping that ignoring the comment would silence my abuser.

It didn't. Within minutes, he started in again—only louder: "YOUR FACE IS GONNA STICK LIKE THAT!"

I walked to the opposite side of the stage. Some of the audience laughed when I did. They could hear the heckler, too. So naturally, I now felt I had to comment on the incident—even though I couldn't see the heckler because the stage lights were blinding me.

My daddy used to say, "Mark, your mouth gets your rear end in more trouble. Your rear end didn't do a thing, but your mouth gets your rear end in trouble. (You know how parents always have to say things twice.)

Well, this particular night, in front of four thousand people, my mouth made a fool out of me, and all my rear end wanted to do was hightail it out of town.

I thought I had the perfect squelch. When I used to speak at public-high-school assemblies, the really "cool" kids would always sit on the front row. Their hair, lips, and fingernails would be dyed, painted, and outlined in black—all black.

And all I could think of was their Avon lady must have been in mourning.

I knew these kids wanted attention or they wouldn't have dressed like they were dressing, so I'd always oblige them. Walking over to them, I'd ask if any of them had passed a mirror today and did anything seem a little odd about the experience. Then I'd look at the audience, and while pointing to those kids, I'd say, "This is what happens to you when your mother takes drugs while she's pregnant."

Everyone would cheer—the other students, the teachers, even the kids in black because they were getting the attention they craved. And those kids usually came to the night's rally.

The squelch always worked with that crowd—worked great, in fact. So while I was standing there on that Gatlinburg stage, I remembered my old comeback line, and thought, "Hey, Mark, that could work here, too."

Forgetting that this was a Gaither crowd, not a high-school assembly, and ignoring the fact that I couldn't see the person I was talking about because the stage lights were in my eyes, I opened my mouth and out flew my perfect squelch.

The side of the audience where the heckler sat sucked air so hard my bridge nearly flew out of my mouth. The laughter that, a second before, had been echoing all over that big auditorium died so fast, turning the place so quiet, you'd have thought we were at a funeral.

Well, I tell you. Sweat started running down the center of my back, like it does whenever I jog out to get my mail.

Something was very, very wrong. And I still couldn't see a thing.

Somehow I finished the monologue then sat down next to Bill Gaither whose face was now paler than the faces of the students dressed in black. I looked at him to get some kind of smile, some kind of reassurance that those groans from the audience were just another form of applause, looking for just a ray of hope that I might get to stay in the Gaither Vocal Band. But his eyes only stared straight ahead. Without leaning toward me, he began to whisper a sad, breathless, almost inaudible whisper: "He's in a wheelchair."

I didn't understand him at first, so I put my ear right over his mouth. He whispered it again.

This time I heard.

And that whisper was the loudest thing I'd ever heard in my life: "HE'S IN A WHEELCHAIR!"

I felt like Arnold Schwarzenegger had hit me in the stomach and left his fist there. The room began to spin. I gasped for breath. My life flashed before my eyes (just the good parts; it didn't take long). I wanted to get up and run. Run as far away from Gatlinburg as I could, wanted the earth to open up, swallow me, and burp ashes.

I live by new rules now. I don't talk to ANYBODY in my audience that I can't see. If I can see a heckler, I'll talk to him. If I can't, he can holler until Gabriel drowns him out with his trumpet. I'm not talking back. (And I won't guide blind people without at least three dress rehearsals, either.)

Now, for my third through twenty-fifth most embarrassing moments . . .

Never mind. This book would become a mini-series.

Flying Down the Road

After my first few years on the road, I quit driving all over the country and started flying. It seemed like the logical thing to do. I work in many different cities, some thousands of miles apart, often in the same weekend. At times I still miss the aroma of an Odessa cattle ranch as I drive down the highway. But, even though I've had my share of bad flying experiences, I've tried to convince myself that flying really beats driving.

I just got home from Denver, for instance. It was to be a two-hour flight that turned into two hours—plus fifteen of the longest minutes of my life. As we were approaching Houston, just feet from the ground, the captain revved the engines and took off again. It was so foggy at the airport that we couldn't see the ground, even though it was only inches away.

As I pulled my heart from somewhere down near my kneecaps and my life flashed before my eyes (and I was thinking about how boring it had been), the captain came on the loud-speaker system and claimed he couldn't land because there was another airplane on our runway.

I thought, don't runways have two lanes? But when I looked out my window, there wasn't ANY runway below our plane.

And I tried desperately to convince myself this beats driving.

Now when I fly, I put all such thoughts out of my mind. There's just not enough room in there for everything. I pretend that pilots, airplanes, landing gear, wing supports, and flight attendants are invincible.

I pretend that dinner flights actually serve dinner when, in reality, the little scraps of food they place in front of us would be rejected by the starving kids in China who, our mothers were always telling us, would kill to eat our vegetables. (If we'd just go ahead and place that stuff directly in the barf bag, we'd really be saving ourselves a lot of time.)

I pretend that connecting flights are actually in the same airport when in reality I'm lucky if they're in the same county.

I pretend that those poor underpaid airline employees really have my best interest at heart when they take one look at me, notice I haven't seen my feet in weeks, decide I need an aerobic workout, and send me running to the wrong gate with three minutes to spare before missing my flight. (That's when I realize I'm darting to my flight down a hallway they call a TERMINAL.)

And I try to convince myself this beats driving.

I try to forget that I'm in an airplane that was built by the lowest bidder.

I strap myself into a seat that reminds me of the time I sat in an electric chair when they threw an open house down at the prison. We climb to thirty-five thousand feet, too high to see the little cars that look like something from a kid's train set, too high to see the first layer of clouds that cover the earth, and I remember the verse in which God promised, "low" I am with you always.

And I try to convince myself it beats driving.

On every flight, the attendants go through the same safety precautions. Some flight attendant with a voice like a billy goat that has a chainsaw stuck in it, tells us where the exits are, tells us how to fasten our seat belts, tells us about our oxygen masks, and then tells us to look at a little card in the seat pocket in front of us that explains all the safety procedures.

While I lean over to look at that card, I see the fellow beside me all bent over in his seat. The guy looks like he is trying to kiss himself good-bye. And I notice they've forgotten to put enough barf bags in my seat pocket.

And I try to convince myself this beats driving.

I can see it now . . . the plane's going down; I've got my seat belt on. (I've always wanted to be strapped to a falling plane). My oxygen mask is glued to my head. I've ripped both the oxygen mask out of the ceiling and the seat from the floor, and I'm trampling everyone in my path trying to remember where that flight attendant put those exits . . . and then . . .

An air pocket startles me from my daydream; I lower my seatback to a more comfortable position, and I try to convince myself this beats driving.

Then the flight attendant sways down the aisle, asking passengers if we'd like headsets. I say, "Sure, what are they? Another safety precaution?"

No, she explains patiently. They're used to listen to music.

I thought, "Well, anything to get my mind off the flight." I take one and immediately turn to a comedy station that's playing the best of Bill Cosby, one of my favorites.

But something is wrong. During the routine, every time Noah is fixing to talk to God, the channel flips over to a country singer singing, "All My Ex's Live in Texas." At first I think Bill just doesn't know his Bible. I try to convince myself that listening to a defective airplane headseat is better than listening to my radio while I'm driving.

Luggage is another thing. My luggage has a mind of its own. Whenever I'm going to Denver, it goes to Detroit. I go to Houston; it goes to Honolulu. I go to Los Angeles; it arrives in Las Vegas.

And a bag never lasts me a year. I remember those television commercials where the baboons were throwing bags around a cage while the announcer's voice stated, "If our bags can withstand this punishment, they can surely handle the airlines'."

HA! HA! HA!

Of course they can—the airlines use baboons to handle the bags! I know, because I found a banana in my shaving kit!

And I take a bite and try to convince myself this beats driving.

After each flight, I always look so good, too. My hair's all greasy, my shoes are scuffed, my hamstrings are sprung, my glasses are on crooked, and my shirt smells tired.

But if I had to drive to Denver, I would still be on the road. It's a two-hour flight or a fourteen-hour drive. From here to L.A. is a three-hour flight or a three-day drive. From here to London is an eleven-hour flight or a long swim.

So I've convinced myself that flying beats driving.

Yes . . . yes, indeed I have. ✗

✗ Point to Ponder: Why don't they make airplanes out of the same material as those little black boxes that always survive plane crashes?

I was flying not too long ago on a full flight. It was packed. I have to fly so much, I wish I could just be faxed over. Especially now that the cheap fares make it easy for everyone to fly. Before that, I could have several seats open around me, so I could relax. You know what I mean—I could loosen my belt and explode. But now, people are in these seats and don't leave me any room to expand.

And sometimes, those people have something worse than airline food. Worse than narrow, bottom-busting airline seats. Worse than carry-on trunks.

They have babies.

I was flying in a window seat on a long flight, and I was praying I'd have an empty seat next to me. At the last minute, the old gentleman sitting on the aisle had been bumped up to first class. I thought, "That's great! I'm going to have both of these seats to myself. I'll get to raise those armrests, grab the pillows and blankets, then lie down and enjoy myself."

But I was not so fortunate. I looked up the aisle and saw *them* coming: A young mother and her six-month-old child.

And they were heading straight toward me.

(Suggestion: Now that smoking is prohibited on all flights, why don't airlines convert the no-smoking/smoking sections into baby and no-baby sections?)

Plop. They settled in. And worse, the baby was going to fly in the seat by me.

I don't have anything against children. I'm single, never married, and I don't have offspring. If you're going to stay single, never get married, and you want to be in the ministry, you really shouldn't be having children.

So I'm not used to kids. I like my nephews and my nieces, but I don't want every other kid around me, because I don't know what to do with them.

And I had no idea what to do with this baby beside me. She sucked on anything she could get in her mouth. She was sucking on the seat belt for a while. Then she got bored with that, saw me, decided I looked edible, and began sucking on my arm. The mother thought it was cute. The hairs on my arm looked like they had been moussed before we got off the ground. I felt like a salt block. I didn't think she was sucking that hard until I noticed two of my tattoos were missing. (How old are humans when they quit this practice? What if, instead of shaking hands, we licked each other?)

The kid just kept sucking.

And then the mother began to talk to me. She was one of these friendly types who talks nonstop. You know, a circular breather. So I just put my book down. I figured I was going to have to talk.

"What do you do for a living?" she asked me. I hate that question, because I have no idea what I do for a living.

I said, "Well, I tell stories about my life from a Christian perspective. I write Christian songs, I sing in a gospel quartet, and I just travel around doing my little thing."

She said, "Oh, that's nice!"

Everything I did was nice. "That's nice. Oh, that's

nice. Oh, that's nice." And she kept talking and talking and talking.

Then, about halfway through the flight, she said to me, "Do you mind if I change her diaper right here? It's only a wet one."

I felt like saying, "Do you mind if I throw up right here? It's only a wet one."

What could I tell her? I'd already told her I was a Christian, so I couldn't tell her what I really thought.

She opened a Pampers box, and I fought the urge to say, "Looky there, you don't have to change her diaper! It says right on the box, up to twenty-six pounds! We can weigh her and keep flying!"

Oh, but no, she wouldn't have it. She opened that diaper, and surprise! Surprise! Surprise! It wasn't just a wet one.

The oxygen masks fell out of the ceiling. I thought they were going to have to raise that wall back up in Germany. It looked like that kid had eaten a whole bottle of Dijon mustard. The guy behind me leaned over and said, "Pardon me, but do you have any Grey Poupon?"

My dad would say, "Mark, you need to learn to watch what you say."

Dad, if you knew what I was editing out, you'd be proud.

I used to sit in the back of the plane.

Know why?

Because I have never seen a plane back into a mountain.

Have you ever seen a plane wreck? The whole plane will be demolished and that tail will be sticking up. I figured if I got my tail on the tail, I'd save my tail.

Then I started getting a little braver and began moving up.

Now, I always get as close to the front row as I can, so if the plane crashes, I'll be killed and not maimed.

I was sitting on the front row the other day, and there was an old lady sitting next to the window. I knew she was old because her teeth were brand-new. She was sound asleep, in one of those coma kind of sleeps. You know, drooling on her pillow.

That's how you know you've had a good night's sleep—when you have to wake up and wring the pillow out in the morning.

Watching her drool, I had this awful urge come over me to just slap the side of her chair and holler, "WE'RE CRASHING!" But I didn't do it, and that's how I know God is still working in my life.

But before I got brave enough to be on the front row, I made it to the exit row.

On the exit row, you've got more leg room, and—an extra special incentive—they don't let children sit on exit rows.

The one thing that bugs me about the exit row is The Seatback Card. The airline attendants are always coming by to say, "Have you read the seatback pocket card?"

Have you ever noticed those cards? In big letters, it says at the top, "If you cannot read this, then please tell the attendant."

What it says in a nutshell is, if the plane goes down I've

got to know how to open that door and help people off the plane.

Did you know that? If you sit on the exit row, that is your responsibility. You've got to know how to open the door and help people off the plane.

I always tell them, "Yeah, I've read it. I'd be happy to stay on the burning plane and escort others off. 'Thank you for flying Delta. Thank you. Watch that first step, it's a doozy!'"

Help people off the plane? I'll help them off the plane. If they can follow my wide rear end going through that door. I may put a flashlight between my legs that they can follow. But, baby, I'm getting off the plane!

X :♡: ♫

The worst thing, though, is getting on the wrong flight. I've done this twice. I'm a college-educated person, and I've not only gotten on the wrong flight, but flown it.

I sing a song about it.

It goes like this:

*Had to catch a plane for Nashville, but was running oh
    so late.*
*Checked my luggage at the curb and prayed the plane
    would wait.*
I passed some Hari Krishnas, racing for Gate 3
The pilot turned the engines on and I yelled, "Wait for me!"
*The flight was overbooked, and there was someone in
    my seat.*

So they put me up in first class, where they get real food
    to eat.
I buckled up, we took off. Things turned out, after all.
'Til then the pilot said, "Welcome to our flight to
    Omaha!"
First class, wrong flight, what a situation.
First class, wrong flight, should have checked the
    destination.
I sat there twenty minutes just deciding what to do.
Guess I could take up skydiving or hijack all the crew.
I thought, "Why should I sweat it? I'll eat my steak and
    smile.
It's not important where I go; I'm going there in style."
First class, wrong flight, what a situation.
First class, wrong flight, should have checked the
    destination.
Style and comfort may be grand, but it's important where
    you land.
Make sure the way you choose is right.
Well, I won't be eating peanuts or hearing some
    kid cry,
I'll have a lot of legroom. It's the only way to fly.
I'll get the royal treatment. Those in coach will envy me.
But when we touch down, they'll all be where they want
    to be.
First class, wrong flight, what a situation
First class, wrong flight, should have checked the
    destination.

✗ FIRST CLASS, WRONG FLIGHT. Lyrics: Tony Wood & Martha Bolton. Music: Phil Madeira. © 1994 BMG Songs, Inc. (Gospel Div.)/Word Music (a div. of Word, Inc.,)/Madeira Whine Music (adm. by Reunion Music)/Bases Loaded Music (adm. by Reunion Music)/ASCAP. All rights reserved. Used by permission.

The Hernia Tour

There are some mysteries about women that I may never be able to solve. Why, for instance, would most women rather go to the symphony than a wrestling match? How can some women shop in every store in town in one day? And why would most women rather watch *The Bridges of Madison County* than *Die Hard IV*? While the answers to these questions may always elude me, there is one I KNOW I'll never understand.

Why do girls carry so many more suitcases than guys when they travel? I had no idea a girl could carry so much stuff until I invited Kathy Troccoli on my Remotely Controlled Tour.

The year before, on my Mouth in Motion tour, there were thirteen guys on the bus: Michael O'Brien, Beyond the Blue (three guys), eight crew members, and me. Each of us brought just one suitcase, leaving us tons of storage space on the bus and in the bays beneath. We had room for tapes, videos, shirts, and other concert products.

But all that changed.

When Kathy arrived on the first day of the new tour, she pulled up in a tractor-trailer. I remember thinking, "Why does a petite, pretty girl like Kathy need a semi?"

When they opened the back of the trailer, I immediately saw why. Neatly piled inside and arranged in alphabetical order (A for accessories, B for bathing products, C for cash), were all 139 of Kathy's suitcases.

THAT'S ONE HUNDRED AND THIRTY-NINE! (Obviously, some letters had more than one suitcase.)

As they were unloading her "freight," I sneaked a peek into one of the cases. It was full of black skirts—short ones, long ones, pleated ones, leather ones, and plastic ones. If they made a black skirt, it was in that trunk. I was unzipping another suitcase when I heard Kathy hollering at me from the front of the bus, so I quickly zipped it shut. (I had to finish my snooping later.)

I don't get it. Why do women need so many clothes? I wear the same pair of blue jeans a week at a time. I can wear the same shirt for two or three days. It always lets me know when it's time for a new one. (Hold on . . . yeah, I got six more hours on this one.) I do change my underwear and socks after I shower. In a pinch, of course, I can always turn 'em inside out and wear 'em another week.

Kathy, though, packs a HAIRBRUSH for every occasion. She's got one that curls, one that frizzes, and one for straightening out the curls and frizzes. Man, she's got the stuff. Her makeup case looks like the cosmetics department at J.C. Penney. When she carries it, she looks like she's either headed to the theater to do makeup for the cast of *Cats* or she's about to do Bond-O work on a totaled '57 Chevy.

I don't need a hairbrush. My blow dryer and fingers do the trick. I don't carry hairspray, either. I didn't need it on that tour, anyway. I'd just sneak into Kathy's dressing room every night before I went on stage and use hers. It's much cheaper, and that way I knew our scents wouldn't clash. Besides, I get a better selection from Kathy's hairspray collection. She carries six different kinds. I think she even has the Ronco "hair-thickening" spray they advertise on TV. But she only uses that when her bald spot is showing.

We finally loaded all the suitcases in the back of the bus and in the bays underneath. You should have seen that bus pull out of Nashville. It was riding so low that we had to get out and push it over speed bumps. All we were missing were the jalapeño-shaped Christmas lights strung around the windows. As we rolled down the interstate, Kathy said with concern, "I hope I didn't forget anything." All I could wonder was, "What could she have POSSIBLY left behind?!"

Then, when we arrived at each new city, you should have heard the way Kathy "Mafia Mama" Troccoli barked orders to our crew. With a growl in her voice, she'd say: "Haul those bags to my dressin' room before I plug ya."

I decided we need to rename the tour the "The Hernia Tour." Or at least "The Happy Hernias."

My next tour is with four women—Point of Grace . . . I think I'll fly.

It seems safer now, somehow, and definitely roomier.

Just Say Thanks

A few years ago I'd just finished a concert and was standing at the back of the auditorium when a little old lady walked up to me.

"That sure was pretty singing," she chirped.

I said, "Thank you, ma'am."

Mark Lowry

Suddenly, the woman's beauty-shop-blue hair was wiggling, her head was shaking so hard. "Oh, no, son," she corrected me, "don't thank me. Just say, 'Praise the Lord.' It wasn't you singing; it was God."

"Oh, no ma'am, it was me," I said. "God can sing a lot better than that."

When I traveled in college with the evangelistic team, every now and then a weightlifter would travel with us. He was one of these big, brawny, bold characters.

He used to tell the audience that he wasn't the one lifting weights but Jesus in his tennis shoes. Some nights he couldn't get the weights up off the ground, and I'd lean over to our piano player and say, "Isn't that something? Jesus can't lift five hundred pounds!"

I heard a story once about a preacher driving through the hills of Virginia. He came upon a little old lady working in her garden on her palatial ranch. He noticed how every bush was beautifully manicured, how the sidewalk was perfectly edged. He stopped to talk to the little lady. He told her what a beautiful place God had given her. She said, "Yes, he has. But you should've seen it when he ran it by himself."

Another time, I was standing with a friend of mine at Estes Park, Colorado, during the Christian Artists Association's "Singing in the Rockies." My friend was complimenting a very well-known Christian artist about a song he'd sung that week. This person said, "Oh, it wasn't me; it was the Lord."

I thought to myself, "Friend, it wasn't THAT good!"

You see, God, who one morning before breakfast, spoke the Word and previously nonexistent worlds began

100

> Talents aren't worth much unless the owner of them keeps plugging.

to spin, CAN lift five hundred pounds off the ground.

The Lord, who invented music, surely can outsing the angels and knows notes Beethoven never heard.

And so, no matter how good we are, we would be absolutely flawless if it were totally God doing it through us. Seems to me, then, it's senseless to say, "It wasn't me; it was God."

God gives talents. But just like the parable of the talents says, what we do with them is up to us. God may have given you a beautiful voice, but if it is going to improve, it's up to you. God may have given you a beautiful piece of land, but he'll never cut the grass or trim the hedges.

And have you ever noticed that most successful people are not always the most talented? Talents aren't worth much unless the owner of them keeps plugging.

If you take a small hammer and keep chipping away at a dam, the dam will eventually break—if you don't give up. Your talent may be a small hammer, a sledgehammer, or a nuclear-powered jackhammer, but the dam will break if you keep chipping.

And then, when you get those compliments, chuck the false humility and shock that little blue-haired lady. When folks tell you they enjoyed your singing or your sermon, your weightlifting ability or your green thumb, a simple thank you is what that person deserves.

My Heroes

The Gaither Vocal Band recently worked on a collection of old southern gospel songs.

The songs were great, but the part I liked the most was singing with the people that made them famous.

Because the guest artists were some of the greatest heroes of my childhood: Dottie Rambo, Jake Hess, Hovie Lister, Howard and Vestal Goodman, Eva Mae LeFevre, George Younce, J.D. Sumner, and Glen Payne—and that's naming just a few.

When I told Mama we were going to do this album of old songs, she said it would sell a million. (So everybody better go out and buy one because Mama hates to be wrong.)

My earliest recollection of southern gospel music was when I was eleven years old. The church I was raised in sang very little southern gospel music. Most of our music was written by John W. Peterson. Straight by-the-book, on-tempo, Baptist singing.

And I was doing a lot of singing by then.

Mrs. Holland would, when I was at my most hyper, tell me to get up in front of the class and sing.

And I was knocking 'em dead at church socials with my imitation of Louis Armstrong singing "Hello, Dolly."

That gave Mama an idea.

And when Mama has an idea, stand back.

She read in the paper about auditions for the Houston Music Theater. They were casting for *The Music Man*, so she packed me in the car and took me straight down there.

Pointing to the stage, she said, "Mark, go up there and do Louis Armstrong." So I did. And I got the part. I made thirty-five dollars. I signed autographs and had a great old time. No longer was I Mike Lowry's little brother. *He* was Mark Lowry's older brother.

Next thing I know I'm doing another show and another. I was a big star.

Mama, though, was getting a little worried. I was liking the theater a little too much. And there was this small problem. All these shows had a lot of dancing in them. And we didn't do that. We were Baptists. We were independent, fundamental, Bible-believing, Bible-banging, foot-stomping, soul-winning, door-knocking, pew-jumping, devil-chasing, sin-hating, King James Version-only Baptists. So I wasn't ABOUT to get to dance. I had to stand there and sing while everybody else was dancing all around me.

The last part I won was in *Oliver*. But, suddenly, in the big, fat middle of rehearsals, the theater went bankrupt.

I always figured Mama's praying did that. Being worried about how well I was taking to the theater, she had already started praying that God would open some other door.

And when that theater went belly up, Mama got another idea. And that door looked wide open: A southern gospel quartet singing was in town.

I had never heard that kind of singing because my daddy hated all that clapping to the music those people did. But Mama saw it as a sign from God.

She took me down to the Jones Hall auditorium in Houston, Texas, sat me on the front row, and waited.

Soon the emcee introduced the Singing Rambos.

I'll never forget it as long as I live.

Buck, Dottie, and Reba came to the stage. Dottie's hair was up in what I call "bedspring curls," pearls going all through them, up, around, down and over. She was playing a guitar as big as she was, singing alto. Reba was pickin' bass and singing soprano. They were flipping parts and pulling against the music, and Dottie was raising that pick every now and then, adding a few words, and shouting.

And when he sang, Buck's lip curled up like Elvis's.

But, oh the sound. I'd never heard anything like it. I didn't know you could slide and slur like that while you sang in harmony. John W. Peterson never did that stuff.

From that moment on I was the Number One Rambo Fan. I started praying that Buck would get sick so I could curl my lip and take his part, singing with Reba and Dottie.

Didn't happen.

Not exactly, anyway.

Next thing I know I'm in Memphis, Tennessee, onstage at the International Song Festival dressed like a flag, all red, white, and blue, singing a patriotic medley that Mama had put together. And who should come by and talk to me but Reba Rambo.

I was in love.

But a Nashville record producer came by, too.

And the NEXT thing I knew, I had a recording contract with a Nashville gospel label, had made two records, one backed by the London Symphony Orchestra and suddenly Daddy, who hated all that clapping to the singing, had bought us a Greyhound bus, scraped "The Inspirationals" off the side, and replaced it with "Mark Lowry and the Impacts."

And I was suddenly doing concerts with the Rambos and the Goodmans and having a great time. (Except I still didn't get to sing with Reba and Dottie. Buck was the picture of health, but I kept on praying.)

Then my voice changed. And it was over.

I got to go back to ninth grade and be normal again.

So when the Gaither Vocal Band started recording the gospel album and those old-timers started warming up for all the slipping and sliding that made them famous, I stood next to Buck while we sang. He was still looking mighty chipper. So I still didn't get to take his place.

And now I have to go practice my Elvis lip curl.

Thankyew, thankyewverymuch.

Showers I Have Known and Loved

Every morning when I'm traveling, I wake up in a new place. And the first thing I do is walk to the shower.

My perfect shower is clear, hard, hot, high, and long.

It's hard to have the perfect shower when you're on the road.

I used to stay in homes. The worst thing about staying in homes is you have to get dressed to go to the shower, because you might meet the lady of the house in the hallway.

105

But now I stay in hotels.

I love hotels. They're private, and best of all you can walk in your underwear from the bed to the shower.

It's amazing how many different kinds of showers there are in our country's hotels. The other day I was in a shower that had a spigot so high I couldn't reach it if I jumped. It felt like I was being rained on, not showered.

Sometimes they're so low all they do is wash my navel good.

Then there are the showers that have several different kinds of massages. These are a joke. If I'm in a part of the country with hard water, the rust freezes the shower on fast massage, and I feel like I'm being bathed by a jackhammer.

Have you ever tried to get the soap off your body when the water is soft? I never can get that nasty stuff off. When I get out of the shower, I have to take my towel and work at it, but all I usually manage to do is move it from one side of my body to the other.

Another kind of shower that I hate is the "water saver." The cheap hotels have them. They look like a little thimble has been attached to the end of the water spigot. They send out such a fine mist, it feels like I'm taking a shower in a fog. By the time the warm water leaves the spigot and gets to my body, it's freezing. The only thing it's good for is being a real good way to catch a cold.

The worst shower I ever had was in Vermont. I was traveling with a few friends from college. We stopped at a motel, one of those mom-and-pop places, and I asked them if they could take a check since we were out of money. They would've taken an IOU. They hadn't seen business in years.

They gave us our key with the big, green, plastic key holder marked with our room number on it. We opened the door and gazed into the room. The beds were swaying enough to be hammocks. They had lost all their support years before.

But the place had a shower.

That was going to make up for everything.

I went first. But when I turned on the shower, a stream of mud came pouring out. I thought the water pressure would soon clear out the mud, and I could continue with a nice, refreshing shower.

But N-O-O-O.

Not only did the mud not clear out, the water pressure dropped. It took five threadbare towels just to get the brown off me.

Now I'm getting to stay in nicer hotels. While I rarely have to shower in mud, not all of THEM are so hot, either.

I stayed in one near the Columbus, Ohio, airport the other day. It was one hundred dollars a night.

When I got up in the morning to take my shower, the room had no running water. They offered to let me take a shower in the workout room. I asked for a partial refund on my one hundred dollars if I had to tromp all the way down there. They said they were sorry, but they couldn't.

I thought, well, I'm sorry but I couldn't stay there again.

They didn't forget the mint, though. Those real expensive hotels always leave a mint on your bed at night when they turn down the sheets. They also leave a little note that says, "You're worth a mint to us."

You bet your sweet bippy you're worth a mint to them. You're paying a mint for your mint.

I never did get that shower. But at least my breath smelled minty clean.

My Secret Diary

I Want to Be a Cover Boy

January 1996

Dear Diary:

Being a big-shot artist, I think it's time I was on the cover of a magazine. Getting on the cover of one of the big-shot Christian music magazines is the ultimate goal for all of us artists. And I've NEVER been on one.

Macho Moped offered me a cover once. But we couldn't agree on the terms. I wanted some sort of payment. So did they.

Buffet Weekly offered me a cover, too. The picture was going to be of me at an all-you-can-eat buffet. But it didn't work out. The photographer got tired of constantly having to restock the serving table for the shot.

And I don't like to brag, but Field & Stream did offer me a centerfold.

But I still haven't made the cover of a Christian music magazine.

Since, as you know, Diary, I write articles for *Release Magazine*, I figured it was my best chance. It's the least you think the magazine could do after all the award-winning columns I've written for them. (*Mama gives out the best awards.*)

So, let me tell you what happened today.

I was talking on the phone with my illustrious editor-in-chief. We were talking about her Christmas vacation, how she had cried all day in airports and airplanes as she winged her way back to Nashville, sad because she had to leave her home in Canada.

As she was sobbing and telling this heartrending tale, I thought it might be a good time to hit her up for a cover.

So between sniffs (*my editor, not me*), I said as sweetly and sympathetically as I knew how, "So, how about a cover?"

She heaved a sigh and said, "Mark, you know it wouldn't be a problem if we were a monthly magazine."

Well, it obviously wasn't a problem for the Newsboys. They got a cover. (*I don't have anything against the Newsboys. They talk a little funny, and some of their costumes make them look like baldheaded baked potatoes, but they're basically good guys.*)

And it wasn't a problem for Amy Grant, either. (*I can sing about my heartbeat, too. It's a little sluggish from trying to pump all that gravy through, but that doesn't mean it's not worthy of a song.*)

But I didn't mention any of that.

Instead, I started sniffing myself and whimpered, "I should have a cover. I deserve a cover. I neeeeeddddd a

COVER."

"*Maybe next year, Mark—or the year after that,*" she mumbled.

"No! I want it now!" I insisted. "*I'm a BIG star! When I go grocery shopping, people are always coming up to me and asking, 'Do you know what aisle the Twinkies are on?' or 'Can you help me find the Ben and Jerry's?'*" "I'm not a nobody, you know!"

"*We realize that, Mark,*" she said.

"*Then, why haven't you offered me a cover?*" I demanded.

"*Okay, Mark, here's the truth,*" she confessed. "*With the size of your head, we'd have to run a special 'foldout' cover, and frankly, we just don't have the budget.*"

So much for my best chance. Time to stalk the other magazines.

Maybe I'll give Field & Stream another call.

FOURTH HALF

Life as a Reluctant Adult

Dental Advice

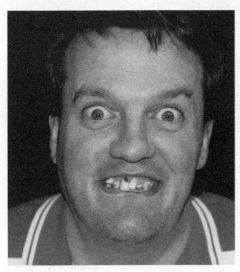

The best Christmas gift I've ever gotten in my life was a set of horrible, ugly, protruding teeth. The wrong teeth are in the wrong places, facing all the wrong directions, and the front tooth—which is about four shades yellower than the others—has a huge cavity at the gum line. I did not find these in Bill Gaither's cup. My brother owned a dental lab for a while and made them for me. And when I put them in my mouth, it just changes my whole personality.

I was ecstatic when I unwrapped them.

See, I'd been waiting for them before I made my first appointment with my new dentist. I'd spent lots of time in dental offices. I got all my teeth capped. They asked, "How white do you want 'em?" I said, "White as they come! I want Chiclets!"

So I wanted to start this new dental relationship off right. I popped the teeth in and headed out. (On my way, I stopped by the Waffle House. The manager took one look at me in my ugly false teeth and asked if I could cook.)

The dentist's office was packed when I burst through the

113

door. Two little kids were playing on the floor, a mother was sitting on the couch reading to a toddler, and two teenagers with braces and acne were talking in the back corner.

And from somewhere in the back, I could hear a drill whining and a kid screaming, "But I used Crest!"

I was in the right place—and I was ready, wearing my upper plate of cavity-infested, plaque-encrusted fake teeth.

Walking over to the counter, I announced loudly (if garbled):

"Hey, I'm Mark Lowry! I've got a 10:30 appointment!"

The way that nurse threw that clipboard at me, you'd think body contact caused tooth decay. She said, "You're going to have to fill this out."

I gave her a big, ugly, toothy smile. "I'll be happy to, ma'am."

A hush filled the waiting room. Little kids were running to their mothers and everyone was looking at my teeth. I went over and sat by the lady reading to her little kid. "I don't know why they make me fill this out," I told her. "I come in here every week."

Nurse after nurse after nurse kept peeking in at me. I'd look up and smile my biggest truck-stop grin. "How ya'll doing?"

One kid couldn't stand it anymore. I was way too interesting to view from afar. He came over and stared straight into my mouth.

"This is what happens when you don't floss, kid," I told him.

Finally, I took out the teeth and announced, "This is just a joke. My brother made these for me."

Laughing, the receptionist said, "Leave them in for the dentist!"

I popped them back in, and she took me ahead of everybody. (Waiting Room Tip: This is how you can get ahead of everybody else at the dentist.) She set me back in the examining chair, stuck a bib around me, and told me she'd send the dentist right in.

When the dentist came, he took one look at me and lost all his oral faculties. You'd have thought I'd shot him with a stun gun.

I grinned big and wide. "Hi, Doc, I've been flossing. I use rope, small chain, anything I can find, but Doc—" I spread my lips wide as I could. "—I think I may have a cavity or two."

He stammered, "Well . . . we can help you, we can help you."

He washed his hands and washed them and washed them. And washed them and washed them. I started to think the guy was headed for the linoleum.

So I took the teeth out. "It's just a joke, doctor."

He fell back against the wall and shook his head. "Man," he groaned, "all I could think about was that I had to put my hands into that mouth."

Everybody ought to get a set of teeth like mine. Because if you eat at Shoney's and tell them you found them in the salad bar, they'll give you a free salad. It works every time.

(Now, I gotta go find my teeth. I've got to get to the Waffle House. I start cooking at six.)

Praying Advice

I am getting old. I'm an adult, if a reluctant one.

All the signs are there. I'm starting to really enjoy cafeterias. And every now and then, when I put my britches on, I have this urge to yank 'em up over my bellybutton.

My grandfather used to walk around like that. I told him if he'd cut that little plastic thing that held his shoes together when he bought them at K-Mart, he could take bigger steps. Before he died he had his britches so high, he had to pull his zipper down to see out.

It's not so bad being thirty-something—really.

It's just that I'm still single.

There are some good things about being single. I don't have to clean out my refrigerator. I've got a piece of celery in there right now that's got longer hair than Crystal Gayle. I can scratch when I itch.

I don't have to share my pizza. I can walk around in my underwear and not offend anybody but my Peeping-Tom neighbors. (And that just serves 'em right.) And I never have to change my sheets. Who cares? When one disintegrates, I put on another one.

I've been reading in the Song of Solomon. Solomon had seven hundred wives. That may sound good, but that meant he also had seven hundred mothers-in-law.

According to some of my friends, I just can't LIVE without that ring on my finger.

But you know what?

Jesus was single.

So when people say, "When are you going to get married?" I say, "Listen, every time you pray, you're praying to a single adult, and don't you forget it."

Bill-Paying Advice

I got a call this morning from a bill collector. Fortunately, he wasn't looking for me. He was looking for someone with the last name of Reiser. This isn't the first time a creditor has called my house looking for this Mr. Reiser. Evidently, when I moved to Nashville, the phone company assigned Mr. Reiser's old telephone number to me.

Evidently, Mr. Reiser didn't like paying his bills.

Evidently, he skipped town, leaving me with his number and his problems.

Mind you, I'm not that fond of paying my bills myself. I used to get so many late notices, my mailman thought "Overdue" was my last name. So, getting chewed out for someone else's debts isn't something I enjoy.

Instead of fretting over it, however, I've decided to have some fun with it.

At first, I told the creditors Mr. Reiser was no longer at this number. They didn't seem to believe me. So now I just say, "Yes, I'm Mr. Reiser."

When the caller inquires about my late payment, I explain that I'd be happy to pay if they'd just lend me some more money.

The creditor is not usually amused.

Then I add, "The stuff I bought wasn't that great anyway, so why should I have to pay for it?"

The creditor tries explaining that's not how the system works.

I say, "That's how it works around here. Stuff not good? Stuff not paid for."

He is still not amused.

The creditor then tries to work out some sort of payment plan for me.

I generously volunteer a quarter a week.

He says that's unacceptable and that he is losing patience. He threatens to ruin my credit rating. I dare him to try.

He hints at taking legal action.

I tell him I'm a personal friend of Judge Wopner.

He tells me I'm being unreasonable.

I tell him I'm going on *Oprah*.

About this time, I lean back in my La-Z-Boy, grab my lemonade, and smile. I crack myself up. This is a blast! It sure beats watching my old videos of the *Jim & Tammy Show*.

What's really fun is coming home after a long trip and having sixteen messages waiting for me on my answering machine—one from my mom and all the rest for Mr. Reiser. (Come to think of it, Mom's last message was for Mr. Reiser, too.)

It's cool being hounded by a bill collector when the debt isn't mine. I don't have to be intimidated or afraid. I don't have to make up excuses or beg for leniency, because it's not my bill.

As for Mr. Reiser? I'm having so much fun, I just might

find out every city he moves away from, move there, and request his old number.

Nose-Hair Advice

I used to love Christmas.

I would stay awake as long as I could, pressing my nose against the window, straining my little eyes for a glimpse of a red nose flying across the sky to my Texas home. Sleep would finally win out, and I'd dream of what was waiting for me under the fake Christmas tree with the leaves that looked like they were made from the same aluminum foil that Mama wrapped the turkey in. Then about 5:30 in the morning, my dreams would come to a screeching halt. I'd jump from the bed and run down the hall to the cry of my mama, hollering from underneath her curlers: "Get back in that bed and wait till I get the eight-millimeter!"

Mama had a thing for capturing our precious memories on her eight-millimeter camera with the lights bright enough to use for landing planes. It took some time to get that rig together.

So I'd wimp back to the bedroom and rouse my brother. We'd sit on the edge of the bed, talking about what I'd seen before Mama ordered me back to my room. "I think I saw one of those battery-operated cars I can ride in. It had my name on it." I'd say.

"Did you see one for me?" he'd ask.

"Nope, but I did see some Barbie dolls with your name on 'em." That would start a wrestling match that would last until Mama and Daddy had turned on that bright light and started the eight-millimeter rolling.

"Come on down, boys!" they'd finally holler, and off we'd go. Our living room looked like Dad had bought Toys R Us. Every inch of the floor was covered. I used to tear into those packages just hoping for something like a G. I. Joe to play with.

Most of the stuff under the tree was what we wanted. But, by a certain age, we could spot the others easily. These were usually packages from the grandparents or other assorted relatives not "in the know." We knew those gifts would be suits or socks or ugly ties or something else totally useless to a little boy. A new shirt? I didn't even finish unwrapping it before I'd be flying across the room searching for another toy wrapped in the gawdy paper with the bow that never really did come untied and the greatly over-taped cardboard box.

I'm not a little boy anymore. The old eight-millimeter is in the closet, and now the video camcorders are the rage. I'm still getting the ugly ties. And I still don't wear 'em. But I don't get toys anymore.

That's not the worst part, though. You really know you're getting old when your mother buys you a nose-hair clipper for Christmas.

There, under the box of Lifesavers Mama has been putting in our stockings every Christmas for as long as I can remember, I found it: A NOSE-HAIR CLIPPER.

I admit when I hit thirty I did notice, occasionally, that

I would have a thin hair peeking out from under one of my nostrils. But I plucked one the other day that had a root on it the size of Texas. And there's nothing more painful than plucking a big-rooted hair out of your nose.

Let me say up-front that I never cry. I can cut onions and never shed a tear. I can watch something as sentimental as *Forrest Gump* and laugh at all the weeping, sub-humans around me. But let me get ahold of a hair in my nose—one that feels more like a paper clip than a hair, one that is so firmly rooted it takes a piece of brain with it when it leaves—let me pluck out that baby, and I start wailing like Tammy Faye at a yard sale.

How is it that something so small, so minute, so insignificant you would never even notice it if you passed it on the street can become the cause of the most excruciating pain known to mankind?

Women may say childbirth is more painful. No, it's not. Giving birth to a baby hurts a little, but at least you get a cute little kid out of the deal. When I pluck one of those curly fries out of my nose, all I get is something I have to flick off my finger.

Pretty gross.

Gross is getting older.

I'm fighting the battle of the "Bs": Baldness, Bifocals, Bridges, Bulges, Bowlegs, and Bunions. I guess hair growing out of my nose is all part of that. I figure if I'm at the age where God wants me to have nose bangs, that's his business. I'm also growing hair out of my ears, too. I may have to start putting shampoo on my Q-tips.

But that's another story.

So I guess it's good I don't get toys anymore. Mama was

121

pointing out an inevitable fact of life. When you're a kid, you don't have hairs growing out of your nose. When you grow older, you have more things to take care of. You don't have time for toys—you have to shampoo your ears and pluck your nose weeds.

So, when something's tickling your upper lip and it's not a moustache, be prepared. A nose-hair clipper may be waiting in your stocking, too.

(It'll be in the box that's wrapped the fanciest. That's the way it always is, you know. When you're grown-up.)

Eating Advice

I love to eat. My favorite food is Mexican food. I was raised in Texas, and Texas has the best Mexican food in the world. Texas has better Mexican food than Mexico does.

But when you're in Texas and you're looking for a good place to eat Mexican food, never ask a skinny person. Skinny people are no fun. They're usually miserable. You know why? Because they're hungry! Fat people are more fun, and they always know the best places to eat.

I spoke at a banquet not long ago. The group was great, but the food stunk. They fed us a steak, a baked potato, a salad, and some sort of moon-shaped, orange-colored vegetable they placed right between the steak and the potato. I had never seen a moon-shaped orange-colored vegetable in my life. So I bit into it, and I'm here to tell you, it was nasty! It sort of crunched, and it had NO flavor.

I asked them what it was.

"Sweet potato," they informed me.

"Sweet potatoes aren't supposed to crunch," I told them. "Doritos are supposed to crunch. Sweet potatoes are supposed to come out of the oven on Thanksgiving morning with marshmallows on top of them, nuts down the sides, juice all through them, and some unknown liquor substance my Mama sneaks into the house at Christmastime over them."

"Oh, but it's healthier this way," they explained.

Healthier, huh? That is the stupidest thing I've ever heard of. In my opinion, vegetables were not meant to crunch. Broccoli, for instance. It's not supposed to be crunchy; it's supposed to be cooked so long it almost turns yellow. Then it's supposed to have cheese sauce poured all over it to disguise the ugly yellow color.

I was up north once and got into a discussion about food with a pitifully healthy-looking lady. "Oh, we don't overcook our vegetables up here," she said. "We don't want to cook the vitamins out of the vegetables."

"For goodness sakes," I told her, "take a pill and cook the vegetables!" You ever bite into a vitamin pill? They taste awful. You know why? Because they've got vitamins in them. That's why you need to cook those vitamins right out of those vegetables. They'll taste better. Forget the health nuts. We're all gonna be dead in a hundred years, for goodness' sakes. COOK THE VEGETABLES!

Fat, greasy, crunchy, you fry it, I love it. I want my

blood going through my veins saying, "Excuse me, pardon me, coming through, pardon me."

I want mashed potatoes with a lake of gravy in 'em. And leave the skin on that chicken. Don't make that bird die in vain—fry that chicken!

Put the sugar in the tea; that's where it goes. Not that pink stuff that causes cancer. I like my tea so sweet that if I run out of syrup, I can pour it over my pancakes.

And don't put sugar in my cornbread, either. That is not of God. Sugar in cornbread is cake. When you bite into cornbread, it's supposed to suck 90 percent of the moisture out of your body.

And then, whatever you do, don't exercise all those fine calories off! Like I said, I do one sit-up a day. I get up in the morning. That's half. I lie down at night. That's the other half.

I figured out a long time ago, my body is for nothing more than carrying my head from place to place anyway.

Diet Advice

Considering the way I eat, you've probably figured out by now that I have a constant battle of the bulge.

I hate diets. I've been on most of them, because I've been overweight most of my life. In fact, sometimes I feel like I was born to eat. My problem is I love all the wrong foods. I love fried, greasy foods so much that in many restaurants I've been tempted to order just a bottle of Crisco and a straw. **X**

Being reared in a Christian home, I've been subtly taught that the only vice that's acceptable is to eat and eat good. You go to church, you go to the grocery store, and you eat. Then, if the Lord calls you into a traveling ministry like mine, nearly all of your meals are in restaurants. Of course, there are salad bars in nearly every one of these restaurants. And that's fine if you're a rabbit. But how many rabbits do you know who cover their greens with ranch dressing?

And how about those carrot sticks dipped in blue cheese?

That's my kind of bunny.

I've been on every kind of diet known to mankind. I've been on the powdered-drink diets that taste like liquid chalk. I've been on the high-protein, all-meat diets, which are great if you're a vulture. I've been on them all, and they all work. I'm proud to say I've lost three or four hundred pounds on diets. Problem is, I always find them again.

Ever notice that when you're on a diet, TV commercials take on a new life? I can nearly smell and taste that junk food on those commercials for Hardee's, Burger King, Wendy's, and Taco Bell. It's embarrassing, but a few times I've caught myself on all fours down by the TV, licking the screen.

And the billboards. I never notice billboards until I'm on a diet. Then they become 3-D. Get two people on a

X When you burp, can you play Name That Meal?

125

diet driving by a Burger King billboard, and fenders are going to bend.

But the worst thing is when I pass my favorite restaurant. The car swerves without my permission. It's true. Some demonic force takes over the wheel. It wasn't my fault I parked, went inside, and chowed down. I didn't even want to eat that salad bar! But suddenly I'm telling the waitress: "Forget salad plates—they're too small. Just hand me a FORK!"

Have you ever noticed that you hardly ever hear preachers preach on gluttony? That's because most of them are fat, too. They'll preach on every other kind of overindulgence, but leave the groceries alone. A lot of fat preachers used to wear vests with buttons bulging, ready to pop off and wipe out the whole front row of their church. (Which is a great idea if you have a problem with one of your deacons and can aim properly.)

We've been trained in this country to live to eat, rather than to eat to live. Our bodies weren't made for this kind of punishment. It's very hard for people to take seriously a speaker or minister's messages against drinking, smoking, and drug abuse when, at the beginning of a service, they watch one of us walk from the pew to the pulpit and notice our stomachs are getting rugburn.

Some people have a very real physical problem that causes them to be overweight, but they are few and far between. Most of us just live for that next calorie.

Whenever I've been confronted in the past about my weight, I've laughed it off. When a friend who hasn't seen me for a while notices I've gained a few extra pounds, I've quipped: "It's all paid for!"

Or: "I'm not finished yet!"

I do a great impression of a waterbed.

This morning Seaworld called me. They said Shamu the killer whale was sick and asked me if I could swim.

I told them I was booked.

Okay. Okay. It's not funny anymore. I think it's time to do something.

The only way I'll ever lose weight is to declare war, a LIFETIME WAR. For people like me it's not a week-long fast, it's a lifetime commitment—a day at a time—a meal at a time—moment by moment.

Where are those carrot sticks?

I'm hungry.

And hold the blue cheese. Give it to that skinny bunny.

Free-food Advice

Another problem with being an adult is having to remember to pay for everything, and worse, having to carry money around to pay for it.

My favorite thing to use my money for is food. (I know that comes as a big shock to you by now.)

All my friends are fat. I have no skinny friends. I didn't plan it that way. It just happened. I like people who like to eat. They don't make me feel bad about my own "healthy appetite." (That's what your mom called it in front of other people.)

127

And there's nothing I hate more than missing a meal. I would not make a very good Ethiopian. In fact, if I don't feel uncomfortable, bloated, sleepy, and have sore jaw muscles after a meal, I call it a snack.

But the other morning I was reminded that people don't let you eat unless you have money to swap for the privilege.

I actually woke up fifteen minutes before the alarm went off. I had to catch a Delta flight to Farmington, New Mexico, which meant catching an early flight to Phoenix and changing planes.

When I left the house, I thought I had everything I needed. I packed the night before because I never trust myself to pack early in the morning. It's amazing what you can forget to pack when you're half-asleep.

So by 7 A.M. I was driving through Chick-fil-A to get my usual two chicken biscuits and a large lemonade. I pulled around to the window, reached for my wallet, and realized packing the night before doesn't always work.

I had no wallet.

Therefore, I had no money.

I checked the change purse I keep in the door pocket of my car. It had $2.05 in it. It wasn't enough. I apologized to the lady and sped away.

Embarrassed.

And, more importantly, still hungry.

I didn't have time to go back for my wallet. So when I got to the airport, I rode the underground train to my terminal then went to the bakery counter and asked how much a cinnamon roll was with tax.

I was ten cents short. Ten lousy cents! And what made it so embarrassing was what I did after that.

I stood there, in front of people, counting nickels, dimes, and pennies, looking fittingly miserable, in the hopes that someone would have pity on me and offer to buy me one.

(It didn't work. Have you noticed that very few people have sympathy for fat people missing a meal? I mean, what do they think? We can live like hibernating bears off the fat? Well, maybe, but that's only during winter!)

Then, as my stomach continued gnawing on my backbone, it hit me. I'm a member of the USAir Club. For frequent travelers, the USAir Club is a haven in the middle of noisy, crowded airports. And they have FREE sweet rolls.

I had breakfast waiting for me—free.

I placed my insufficient funds back into my pocket, told my squatty legs which direction to take my empty stomach, and headed toward the endless supply of sugar-coated satisfaction that was waiting just around the corner.

There's a life lesson here. Don't forget your billfold, and if you do, don't forget where the free food is.

There's a spiritual life lesson, too. As I chowed down and my senses came back to me (and I remembered again why I'm not the fasting type), I realized I was trying to buy something that was already paid for. That's what I keep doing in my Christian life, too. I'm scurrying around everywhere looking for a little approval, a little nourishment, with very little change in my pocket, when my seat at the table has already been purchased. My ticket to the banquet has been bought. And the cook has made sure there's enough for me.

And all of it is mine to gulp down—FREE.

Fasting Advice

The other day I fasted. I had never fasted before. (Except for that one time I got in line behind my sixth-grade teacher, Miss Barth, at an all-you-can-eat buffet.) But I was praying about some decisions I had to make, and a friend suggested I try fasting.

The fast got off to a great start. I felt strong. I felt energetic. I didn't even miss food.

But then that second hour set in, and I nearly died.

My stomach started rumbling and grumbling, and I soon found myself adding Kentucky Fried Chicken and Taco Bell to my prayer list.

My intestines were making so much noise, the neighbors were starting to complain (even more than they complained when I sold my new video door-to-door). In an effort to take my mind off all this, I decided to do what all Americans do when they're under stress.

I went shopping.

Take it from me, it's not a good idea to go shopping when your brain is suffering from severe vitamin deficiency, because I soon found myself the owner of a brand-new motorcycle. I still don't know why I bought it. I have enough trouble keeping a four-wheeled vehicle on the road. Every year when it snows, I take my car out of the garage and just park it in the ditch. I figure it saves me time since that's where it always ends up anyway.

> Never eat more than you can lift.
> —Miss Piggy

For the record, I didn't buy one of those Harley Davidsons like Bruce Carroll and Wayne Watson have. I bought a small one, the kind I can take on the interstate but don't have to change gears (a wheel or two and maybe an engine after it falls out, but no gears). It's just a little automatic motorcycle.

Actually, it's not even a motorcycle.

It's a moped with an attitude.

Picking out which motorscooter I wanted wasn't as difficult as finding a helmet to fit my head. When I tried on the extra-large, it looked like a thimble sitting on an orange. I tried the extra-extra-large next. But after two minutes, my forehead went to sleep. (I guess it figured my brain had been doing it all these years, so why not join it?)

I finally asked the clerk if he had anything larger. While he contemplated gutting a Volkswagen Beetle and strapping it to my head, one of the other clerks came upon an XXXL helmet that fit perfectly—as long as I shampoo my head in butter first.

My first encounter with one of these little scooters took place

in the Caribbean. Over there, scooters are for rent. I was with nine of my friends, and we all decided to take an afternoon ride together, so we all rented scooters. Unfortunately, one friend rode her bike straight through a plate-glass window at the ice-cream parlor where we had stopped for some refreshments. (I told my friend there were better ways to get the waiter's attention.)

I shouldn't talk. I didn't fare much better on my moped. I took a wrong turn and ended up doing fourteen somersaults down a hillside. (That was the first time anyone had ever called me a "holy roller.") Those who saw me go down said their concern for my safety gave way to laughter when all they could see was my giant helmet bouncing down the hill . . . knocking over bushes, trees, a building, small children . . .

Fortunately, I didn't get hurt. I had some grass stains on my teeth, but that was about it. And for the next few weeks whenever anyone asked me, "What's shakin', Mark?" I had to say, "All four cheeks and a couple of chins." But other than that, I was fine.

Don't let Mama know I got a scooter. I haven't told her yet, so just keep your mouths shut. She can't take much more. She was on her knees for most of my childhood just praying I'd get through it. Her knees can't handle my second childhood.

And what if she gets real concerned and SHE tries fasting?

I don't think I can bear to see Mama popping wheelies on a Suzuki!

Driving Advice

I got another ticket the other day. It wasn't for speeding. It was for running a red light. I was stopped at the light, then I made the mistake of looking in my rearview mirror.

There sat a policeman.

"Oh, no," I thought. "He's going to see I don't have my seat belt on." So without thinking—and I have no idea why—I stepped on the gas.

I blew right through that light.

Right in front of that surprised cop.

He pulled me over.

"Did you realize you just ran that red light?" he said.

"No, I didn't." Which was the truth. I was too busy thinking about my seat belt.

"Didn't you hear all those people honking at you?" he asked.

"Yes," I answered.

"Well?" he asked.

"Well," I said, "I didn't think much about it because I know a lot of people around here."

He didn't much care for that answer, because he started writing a ticket right away.

It reminded me of the time I got a speeding ticket in Dallas. The officer asked me if I knew why he stopped me.

"You don't know?" I asked. "Well, I don't either."

Mark Lowry

Housecleaning Advice

Another thing about being an adult is you don't have a mom around to clean house.

This can become a problem.

But only if someone notices.

I've lived alone ever since I graduated from college. I like it.

Because I never clean my house.

Have you ever noticed all the useless household products they advertise on TV?

Do people really buy that stuff? For instance, that spray used to dispel static cling in the laundry. Who would want to do that? I like static cling. I don't know how to use my fireplace, and that crackling sound and all those tiny sparks make a great substitute.

Carpet cleaners? I don't need 'em. Sure I vacuum—annually. But only on odd years.

Lemon Pledge? That's another one I don't need. The depth of the dust on my desk is my filing system. The only Pledge I use is that I pledge to clean my house when the fire marshal makes me.

I hate cleaning the house. Window cleaners? Who needs 'em? When I bought my new house I thought I was going to have to buy blinds. But I found out that if I never clean the windows, I don't need blinds.

Toilet-bowl cleaners? Nope. Just buy black toilets. I've even learned how to save on laundry soap. I don't buy it. If I take my clothes and run 'em in the dryer long enough, they'll smell good again.

I'm always getting flyers on my mailbox for "Martha's Meticulous Maid Service." Or "House Dirty? Call Myrtie."

Can you believe people actually pay strangers to clean their houses? Who would want strangers to see the mess they've made? Not me. I ask friends to do it.

When I was growing up, Mama always had a maid. The same one for most of my childhood. Her name was Mattie Zahn. She was a six-foot-tall German woman with a gap between her two front teeth wide enough to drive a truck through. She thought our house was her house when she was cleaning it. She'd get on her hands and knees and scrub our kitchen floor. My brother and I would come running into the house about the time she'd finish, and Mattie would cuss us out in German. Daddy wanted to fire her, but Mama said, "No, Charles, those kids don't know German."

When we were not muddying her floors, Mattie would call us, "Honey darling mine." She always smelled like liquid bleach.

I was sitting in my house the other day looking at a stack of mail on the end table, a pile of laundry on the floor, and mud stains on the carpet. I was wondering where Mattie was.

Boy, do I need her. ✗

I still don't know German.

✗ Old Confusion Saying: "If it moves, clean it."

135

Vacation Advice

A few years back, my brother had the great idea for our family to take a skiing vacation. We agreed to go to Snowshoe, West Virginia, about four hours from Lynchburg, where I lived at that time.

I leased some skis, and I borrowed a ski suit from a fat friend of mine.

I looked like the Pillsbury Doughboy in a Hefty bag.

When we hit the slopes, I asked my brother, "Where do I take my skiing lessons?"

He said, "Skiing lessons? Mark, you don't need skiing lessons. Haven't you seen the skiers on TV? You just get out there and keep your balance and head down the hill as fast as you can go."

I should have known I was in trouble when the only skier I remember from television was the one wiping out in the "agony of defeat."

So there I was, standing at the top of the steepest slope I'd ever seen, eyes closed, asking God to let me miss the trees bordering the tiny path I was supposed to slide down.

That is, if I could actually make myself start.

But then I didn't have to worry anymore.

My brother pushed me—way before I was ready. About three years before.

Zooming down the trail, I was jumping hurdles, dodging children, doing a lot of praying (I thought I might as well, since I was already on my knees), I was leaning this way, that way, and everywhichway, but by some miracle of gravity—I DIDN'T FALL OVER!

Those sticks with the pointed ends were helping a little bit. (They helped me jab at the mounds of snow, dodge a few trees, and poke a few folks out of my way.

I was flying past other skiers, wimps taking their time swishing from side to side down the hill, screaming all the way down.

Then I realized I was the one screaming.

About halfway down the slope, I thought to myself, "This isn't so bad. I should've done this years ago."

Right.

The truth was, my eyes were watering, my contacts were stuck to the backside of my skull, my nose was frozen, my joints were aching, and the sting of snow was cracking my lips.

Why, I hadn't had this much fun since my last tumor surgery!

When I finally got to the bottom of the hill, I started looking for the brakes.

That's when I realized I had forgotten to ask my brother that rather important question.

Where WERE the brakes on skis?

Then I found out.

The brakes were the people right in front of me, standing in the ski-lift line.

"Excuse me" (WHAM!!), "Pardon me" (SLAM!!), "COMIN' THROUGH!!!" (POW! WHACK! THUD!).

I lay there in a big pile of wet snow with the breath knocked out of me, my ribs cracked, my poles and skis pointing every direction but right, wishing I was on the beaches of Hawaii getting a good, ordinary, third-degree sunburn.

When I finally got back up the hill, I hobbled to our cabin and immediately began procedures to disown my brother.

It was either that or go back the next year and push *him* off the mountain this time. ✗

But I figure he'd be onto me.

Exercise Advice

Who invented exercise? Why do our bodies need it? Mine has done just fine without it for over thirty years. I know our bodies are the temples of the Lord, but show me where Jesus ever jogged. We have no record of the Lord doing sit-ups. None whatsoever. Everywhere in the Bible that it talks about the Lord's mode of transportation, it says he either walked or rode a donkey.

Jesus didn't RUN on the water. He walked on the water.

Paul said that physical exercise profiteth little. I agree with him. Everytime I've ever exercised, it profited very little.

All right, I'll admit it. I did try jogging once. I went all out, too. I bought some very expensive sweats. I spent ten

✗ Old Confusion Saying: "A bird in the hand is safer than one overhead."

to fifteen dollars on the tennis shoes alone. I even bought a sweatband for my head. What I needed was a sweatband for my body. I hate to sweat.

That fateful morning, I put on my sweats, tromped outside, and tried to jog around the block. I did okay for the first forty-five seconds. Then my heart started racing. My heart hadn't felt like that since I ran the thirty-six minute mile in high school.

(That was probably the *Guinness Book of Records* entry for the event. By the time I came in from that race, all the other kids had showered, shaved, and were halfway home.)

Still, I was out there—jogging. Blisters were forming inside those ten-dollar sneakers, and I figured my heart was supposed to feel like it was pumping blood for the whole county. By the time I'd gotten to the third house down from mine, my sweatpants, sweatshirt, and sweatband were totally soaked with sweat. All I needed was a bar of soap, and I could've skipped the shower. Then my side started feeling like someone had snuck up behind me and stuck a hot poker into it.

I doubled over somewhere near house number four.

Through my legs, I saw some little kids waiting on the school bus. There was one little snotty-nosed kid smacking his lips. He was pointing at me, saying, "Hey, maybe that guy'll drop dead, and we can try out the CPR we learned yesterday at school!"

I gave him the dirtiest look I could muster, the same one I'd been giving everything since I left my house.

When I finally got back home I put my tennis shoes away. I haven't seen them since. I threw my sweatpants in the corner of my closet. They're still standing there. My sweatband has crystallized and is making a nice salt block for the neighbor's cat.

I haven't totally given up on exercise.

My dad's always said he was gonna start jogging just as soon as he passes a jogger with a smile on his face.

I've seen those beautiful bodies on the talk shows. And I must admit those people look really good. But when they're asked how many hours a day they spend in the gym, the answer is always two to three hours every single day!

Who has two to three hours a day to spend in a gym? I certainly don't.

Instead, I just tuck that extra fat roll deeper into my pants. It may be getting harder and harder to hold in my stomach, but it doesn't take two to three hours a day.

Yet.

Surgical Advice

I've had two tumor surgeries in my lifetime.

The first one was on my thyroid.

I didn't even know I had a thyroid. I asked the doctor what it was, and he said it was right here. And then poked my throat (hard). When I'd swallow, it would move up and down.

He said, "It's got to come out, because it's probably malignant, which means you could die if you don't get it out of there. But," he added (and don't you just love those "buts"?), "I should tell you that before we remove it, your laryngeal nerve runs down through there, and if I sever that nerve, you'll never make another noise." Then, he finished this nice pronouncement with a supposedly reassuring note: "Of course, I've done many of these surgeries, and I've never severed one of those nerves."

"Well," I thought, "you're probably about due, aren't you?" But what I said was, "Doctor, you sever that nerve, and when I wake up, YOU'LL never make another noise."

He took the tumor out, and I remember distinctly waking up in the recover room going, "Mi-mi-mi."

I was making NOISE. I had my nerve.

Then they found a parotid tumor on the side of my face. It's the kind that just keeps on growing until eventually I'd have another head on my shoulder. I could draw a face on it and sing a duet.

Guess what the doctor said: "Mark, your facial nerve runs down through there."

You know, there's always a nerve in the way. And guess what the doctor added.

You got it: "I should tell you before we remove it, that if I sever the nerve, the side of your face will be paralyzed."

And it would be the face I was stuck with forever. Not that I'm so great looking now, but I figured that would be worse. I could just see it. My next album cover would be *He Touched Me* with a whole new meaning.

But that story has a happy ending, too. I went through

"Never go to a doctor whose office plants have died."—

Erma Bombeck

---

the surgery fine. In fact, I even came out with a dandy practical joke.

I learned from my first surgery that the last thing you think of before you go under the anaesthesia is the first thing you think of waking up.

So listen closely, children. You can use this on your next surgery.

I planned ahead. I thought and I thought and I thought as they put me under. And when I woke up, the doctor was staring me right in the face. "Smile for me," he said.

And I did exactly what I had thought about right before I went under the gas. I did my rubber lips face contortion. You know the one. That's the face I do (my great talent) where I stretch my lips at a forty-five-degree angle one way and make my mouth look like it's falling off my face the other.

And as I was stretching it as far as it would go, I said: "Mmmggmmwhat happened? Did yoummgggsever my nerve?"

Too bad I was too groggy to see the surgeon hit the floor.

But I'm mighty thankful. My face today is still the perfect creation it has always been. MmggmmmSeeeee?

Parenting Advice

I don't have any kids. The only person who gets a 2:00 A.M. feeding at my house is me. I have no one to blame my outrageous telephone bills on except Yours Truly.

There are plenty of times when I wish I had kids. When I'm stuck entertaining company who've long over-stayed their welcome, I'd love to be the proud father of a four-month-old with colic.

When I'm lying on the couch and the remote control is across the room, what I wouldn't give to have a toddler around to toddle over and get it.

And when I'm standing in a long line at the grocery store, a six-year-old with chicken pox could be just the ticket to get me waited on faster.

Sometimes I even find myself wishing I had teenagers—like when it's time to clean out the refrigerator or when my blood pressure's running a bit too low.

I know kids are great to have around because of the week I just spent with my brother. My brother has two boys, two girls, and a wife. (It's easier to have kids when there's a wife around. And a whole lot more scriptural.)

My brother has this fatherhood thing down pat. He's ingeniously devised a way to "trick" his seven-year-old Christopher into doing all his fetching for him. Take one night when I was visiting, for example. The adults were sprawled out on the sofa downstairs when my brother suddenly decided he'd like a pillow.

"Christopher," he said, excitedly. "Hurry! Go get me a pillow." Then he began to count, "One, two, HURRY, three, four, BETTER HURRY, five, six . . ."

Before he could get to ten, Christopher had run upstairs, grabbed a pillow off the bed, and returned, out of breath.

"I'm (gasp) fast!" he said, beaming with pride.

My brother looked over at me and said, with a smirk on

his face, "They'll do anything if you make a game out of it."

Quite content, he settled back on his pillow and continued to watch television.

A little while later I saw him trying to train two-year-old Chad to follow in his brother's footsteps. "Chad," he coaxed, "Hand me that remote control. One, two, HURRY . . .

Chad just looked at him.

"Three, four, HURRY . . ."

Chad still didn't budge. He didn't move a muscle. I could hear ol' Chad-boy thinking, "Get up off your blessed assurance and get it yourself. This playpen potato's not falling for that old trick." (Obviously, this child is my clone.)

But Chad didn't get into any trouble for not getting the remote, nor did Christopher win anything for getting the pillow. It was just a game. Other than the sheer joy of beating the count of ten, there were no rewards.

I am afraid, though, that one of these days Christopher is going to grow up and realize he has been tricked into doing all of his dad's fetching. By then, he'll probably be an executive at IBM. His boss will ask him to pick up some important papers from the president's office and bring them to a meeting. But Christopher will just stand there motionless. A glazed look will come over his face.

"Well," the boss will snap, "what are you waiting for?"

Just as he's about to be fired, Christopher will straighten his tie, adjust his five-hundred-dollar suit and ask, "Aren't you going to count?"

✗ ☺ ♫

A few months earlier, I had another valuable insight about children on a surprise visit home.

I decided to fly to Lynchburg, Virginia to visit my family. I only told my sister I was coming so she could pick me up at the airport. I surprised everybody else. It was a lot of fun.

They squealed.

Even my quiet dad squealed. Well, it was actually more of an excited grunt, but we'll go ahead and call it a squeal.

When I got off the plane, my sister and my two nephews were waiting for me.

Melissa, my sister, didn't tell Christopher and Chad who they were picking up. They acted so excited to see me.

But then, when we got in the car Christopher informed me that I had forgotten his birthday. He thinks I'm rich and that his rich uncle should never forget his birthday.

Courtney, my niece, had a piano recital at two o'clock. So I told Christopher as soon as the piano recital was over, I'd go and get him a birthday present.

The kid knows persistence. "Can't we go by Toys R Us on the way to the piano recital?"

"We don't have time," I said.

But that didn't deter him. He pointed at the store as we drove by. "There it is. We could just stop. It won't take long." When Christopher gets something on his mind, he doesn't let up. You can never promise him anything unless you're ready to do it right then.

That's when he began to get on my nerves. He wouldn't talk about anything but my missing his birthday . . . what he wanted . . . when can we go? How long is this dumb recital gonna take? What was I gonna buy him?

Finally, I said, "Christopher, if you mention it one more time I'm not going to get you anything for your birthday."

That stopped me. I was hearing words come out of my mouth that had a far too familiar ring to them.

Seems I'd heard them before—many, many years ago. Repeatedly.

I felt like such an adult.

So I tried something. I asked Christopher if he remembered what I bought him the month before when he and his family were visiting me in Nashville. (I'd spent sixty dollars for two video games he just couldn't live without. They were his favorites. To hear him tell it, they'd make his little miserable life truly worth living.) "No," he said.

This was not the right answer.

So I began to cry. (I was actually laughing, but he didn't know the difference.) "You don't REMEMBER? You've already forgotten? I spent sixty bucks, and you can't REMEMBER???"

He started racking his little brain at this point, trying his best to remember the trip, much less the video games.

Now I put it into high gear. "I can't BELIEVE I buy you gifts, toys, and presents, and you don't even REMEMBER them (sob). I spend my hard-earned money. I work my fingers to the bone. I break my back for you kids (heave) (sniff) (snort), and what do I get? 'Give me more!'"

I was really getting into this. My arms were flailing, my

head was spinning; I was having a really wonderful time. Mama would have been proud.

Christopher, at this point, rolled his eyes. "You don't work your fingers to the bone. You hold a microphone and tell jokes."

The boy is smart. He quickly changed the subject. "Well, you surprising us and flying in is a good enough birthday present."

"Nice move, kid," I thought. And then I said, "Thank you Christopher. That's sweet of you."

His response? "You know what I want for Christmas?"

It was amazing. At that moment I thought I heard God speak to me. It wasn't an audible voice; I'm Baptist, after all.

But it was like God spoke to me and said, "See what I go through? How about a little gratitude every now and then?"

You got it, God.

Now, would you talk to Christopher?

Dinner-Party Advice

A friend of mine called me a few months ago and asked if she could throw a dinner party at my apartment for some of her friends who are contemporary Christian singers here in Nashville. She wanted to present an opportunity for Christian singers to minister in Russia.

So Lynn had a fabulous dinner catered by a company here in town. It was very fancy. There were three people in tuxedos to serve the dinner.

When the time came, though, none of the guests had arrived.

We thought, well, they are gospel singers. They must be running a little late.

We waited. We waited. And we waited.

About an hour after everyone was supposed to show, we started getting a little nervous. Folks were standing around my apartment who had come all the way from Russia to present these opportunities to the Christian contemporary music community. Yet no one from that community was crossing town to show up. So we decided to go ahead and sit down at the table, hoping that would make them come.

But that just made it worse. There we were, five of us, at a table for sixteen with enough food for twenty.

So I got on the phone and started calling different singers I knew. No one was at home. Maybe, we thought, that meant they were on their way. So we waited some more. We nibbled. And we waited.

Finally, I looked over at Lynn and started chuckling. You know that kind of laughter that comes out when you're not supposed to laugh? Like at funerals? It's harder to control it when you're not supposed to be laughing. Every time she caught my eye, she would start laughing, too.

Since I live in a high-rise, I decided I was going to go down the hall and invite people to dinner. The lady right across the hall is Mrs. Pickle. She's a widow. I knocked on her door. She was home. She said she'd love to come to dinner. I knocked on the third door down. Gary, the quiet guy, was home, so he came to dinner, too. And on I went. Walking down the hall and pounding on doors.

It reminded me of the parable Jesus told about another dinner where no one showed up. The host told his servants, "Go out into the highways and byways and compel them to come in so that my house may be full."

I didn't take it to the highway—didn't have to. We found there were lots of people who enjoyed our company and our food—right next door.

And you know what? They learned a lot about Russia, too. Not one of 'em knew all the verses to "Amazing Grace." But we all felt a lot of it anyway.

Singing Advice

(WARNING: Subject of the following chapter may make the author sound old. Proceed at your own discretion and pass me my slippers.)

I have a confession to make: I never liked rock-and-roll music. I hated the sound of a screeching, Fuzzbuster-infected guitar.

Know why? I always liked to hear singers sing.

Pure, piercing, melodic, vibrant singers who lay their heads back and SING!

Not my brother. He liked to hear guitars. Loud, obnoxious, screeching guitars. The more it drowned out the singer, the more he loved it.

Dad used to complain about my brother's music. He never complained about mine. Because he liked mine. It was what he was comfortable with. What he grew up with.

I liked old music. Big bands. Big singers. And big ballads.

My brother liked the Beatles.

Daddy loved when traveling evangelists would come through town and preach against my brother's music. I heard my dad say one time he didn't know if that music was good or bad but he knew what he liked.

What my dad was really saying is he likes what he knows. Daddy doesn't like anything that's loud. It hurts his ears. And my brother's music was LOUD.

Well, you might think I'm about to fill Daddy's shoes with what I'm fixin' to say, and maybe I am.

Maybe I'm getting old. Well, in fact, I am getting old. We all are. It's not a question of "maybe" I'm getting old. I'm definitely headed in that direction. And so, since I'm on my way to senility, if you disagree with what I'm about to say, help yourself. You're getting old, too.

And it's good for old people to disagree every now and then.

I went to church with some friends the other day in their

hometown. It's a nice church. It's a good church. They had a little band that played for the congregational singing. They had a big overhead screen that showed the words to the praise choruses they had chosen for this particular Sunday. They had picked some songs I had never heard before. And I think there's a reason I never heard them before. They weren't very good. The words seemed like they were written by one person and the music was written by another person—at the same time in separate rooms—then they got together and tried to make the two fit.

Ouch.

Being the open-minded person that I am, I was trying my best not to be critical. But I got this incredible headache trying to make myself not be critical. So, there I was, standing up (because they always make you stand up in these churches FOREVER. Then you sit down and then you stand up again, then you sit down and then you stand up again. It's a lot like aerobics). There I was, trying to make sense out of these songs, trying not to be critical, trying to make my headache go away, and trying to keep up with everybody bobbing up and down standing and sitting, all at the same time.

I thought, "Hey, this isn't church—this is work."

I started looking for something to wipe the sweat off my forehead from the workout they'd just put me through. (There's a video idea for you: "Sweatin' to the Praise Choruses.")

Now don't get me wrong. I love praise songs. But I am SURE the Bible says something about singing psalms, hymns, AND spiritual songs.

So why DON'T they?

I was standing there (or was I sitting? Whoops, there we went again—bend those knees), thinking: "Why couldn't they throw an old hymn up there on that screen every now and then?"

The old hymns are good. They're not good because they're old. They're old because they're good. If they weren't good, they wouldn't have lasted all these years. They would have been forgotten by now.

(Hey, I hope in my lifetime I write one song that will last beyond my timely death.)

By the time I was about to start banging my head on the back of the pew to make my noncritical headache go away, they started singing "My Jesus, I Love Thee."

HE-EY-Y. I smiled, perking up. I KNOW this one!

It was like slipping on my old comfortable nightshirt. It just felt right.

I started listening to those words.

I'll love thee in life, I will love thee in death, and praise thee as long as thou lendest me breath . . .

And the tension at the back of my neck started to ease. My headache went away. And do you know what I did? I stood right up, laid back my head, and I SANG.

Scripture-Interpreting Advice

I hate mornings. If I have to be somewhere early, it's easier for me to stay up all night.

I hate getting out of bed. I hate the way my body feels, all stiff and sore.

I hate the way my ear pops off my shoulder like a suction cup when I first wake up.

I hate the way my tongue is glued to the roof of my mouth with that vile green mist just waiting to explode from my lips as soon as I force my tongue from its resting place.

I hate the way it feels like someone has snuck into my room during the night and knitted sweaters for all my teeth.

I hate the way my hair looks like I slept with my head in a vice.

I hate the way the sun pierces through the one place that the bedroom curtain doesn't cover and chases me across the bed all morning trying to push me out from under the sheets.

I hate it when I'm awakened real early in the morning by a phone call.

And I REALLY hate it when the phone rings and I've slept wrong on my arm all night. I defy anyone to answer a ringing phone with a limp, buzzy-feeling, dead arm that just flaps from your shoulder until it has time to wake up, too. I end up knocking the phone to the floor, sending that same dead arm after it, and watching it flop around the phone making all kinds of flaccid-flesh, flapping noises.

And then when I FINALLY get the phone to my ear with my good arm, I've made such a racket, huffing and puffing, that the caller thinks he or she has interrupted something and hangs up.

I do enjoy my rest. When I'm home, though, I try to attend an early morning Bible study at a friend's house. They used to meet at 6:30 in the morning. But after several years of my anonymous complaints and death threats, they moved it to 8:30. There are usually about four of us there. Two of the three guys have real jobs: nine to five. The other is a traveling contemporary Christian music artist, like myself. All of them are married and have kids. So getting up early for this Bible study is no big deal to them. They get up early every day. Small children do that. Their lives are not their own.

The guy who heads the Bible study sometimes forgets that the only day of the week I get up early is on Tuesday. I'm not up at the crack of dawn every morning praying, reading my Bible, exercising, or anything else. (I'm fasting, but I don't think that counts since I was sleeping the whole time.) He has two very small children. He hasn't slept in four years.

So he'll call me on a Wednesday or Thursday morning and ask, "What are you doing, praying?"

Hey, I don't do ANYTHING at 6:30 in the morning, much less pray, I tell him. I really feel doing so would be infringing on Chinese people's time with God.

Well, after a few calls like that, I was starting to feel

pretty unspiritual. I know most Christians are up at 6:30 in the morning praying—at least to hear them tell it. Lots of people seem to think somewhere in the Bible, it says you're supposed to pray at 6:30 in the morning. You may even get extra spiritual brownie points if you get up that early and pray. Or at least these chirpy morning people think so.

Yeah, okay. I know King David said, "Early will I seek thee" in Psalm 63:1. But early to one person is bedtime for another. Let's face it, King David needed to get up early— He was KING. He had a lot on his mind. He had a whole kingdom to look after. My kingdom is all of 1,360 square feet. You don't have to get up real early to mind my kingdom. I think David was thinking more clearly when he wrote Psalm 127:2: "It is vain for you to rise up early." You see, he knew HE needed to get up early, but he wanted everyone else to sleep in.

Isaiah didn't like people getting up too early, either. Isaiah 5:11 says, "Woe unto them that rise up early in the morning."

And Zephaniah was really ticked off when he wrote in chapter 3 verse 7, "I said, Surely, thou wilt fear me, thou wilt receive instruction; so their dwelling should not be cut off, howsoever I punished them: BUT THEY ROSE EARLY AND CORRUPTED ALL their doings." (emphasis mine).

So see?

Oh, you pious gasbags out there. I hear you murmuring! I know you're thinking, "I'll just look up these scriptures to see if Marky quoted them out of context!"

HOW DARE YOU?

Too many of y'all are doing that these days, and it's messin'

155

up some wonderful happiness/health/wealth/riches, and yes, restful theology. You really shouldn't be so picky . . .

. . . and you certainly should never let a comedian interpret the Bible for you.

So, know what I did about my early-rising, early-phoning friend? I finally had to name my bed.

I named it "The Word." Now when he calls I don't have to be ashamed. I don't have to be embarrassed. I just tell him, "Sorry, I can't talk. I'm in 'The Word.'"

FIFTH HALF

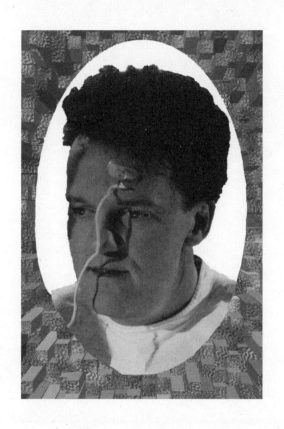

Life as a Profound Philosopher

With All My Liver

Ever been in love? Someone steal your heart?
Ever had your heart broken? Someone stomp that sucker flat?

I was watching the Discovery Channel the other night. I love that channel with all its nature and real-life programming. When helpless little deer are being chased by leopards, and the snakes are eating the chicken eggs, man, I think it's cool. Those animals are always eating better than I am.

Recently, I saw one of the real-life programs that was fantastic. It showed an actual open-heart surgery. Thank God they can do that. If I keep eating Mexican food, I'm going to need it.

They laid a man on the table and put a towel over his head. (I guess that was to keep us from getting sick, in case we knew him.) And then the surgeon cut him right down the middle, ripping his chest cavity apart, exposing everything inside. And we, through the magic of television, could see it ALL. Thump, thump, thump.

The guy's heart looked like living lasagna.

Then they snipped a couple of veins from his legs and sewed them in—to the heart, mind you.

Did you know you have spare parts?

Somehow that doesn't sound right. God doesn't just put veins in you for no reason. That old boy'll probably find out in six months what those veins are for. He's going to be walking down the street with a perfectly good heart, and suddenly, without those veins where God put them, his leg is going to go silly on him all over the street.

For about an hour, I watched the surgeons cut, sew, suture, snip, tuck, and mend that heart. But listen, fixed or unfixed, it is a mess in that guy's chest, and I shook my head.

To think someone would tell another human being, "I love you with all my heart."

If someone said that to me now, I'd probably say, "You love me with your blood-pumping muscle?"

I tell you, it's lost something for me, children.

You know why we say I love you with my heart? Because in Western civilization, the seat of the emotions is the heart.

"I love you with all my heart."

"You broke my heart."

"Put your heart into it."

But not so in other areas of the world. In some lands, the seat of the emotions is the kidneys. In other countries, it's the liver. I'm serious. Ask the next missionary who brings that twelve-hour slide show to your church where the seat of the emotions is in his or her country.

In some countries the seat of the emotions is the liver. In some—the kidneys.

Somewhere tonight, in some other language, a guy's telling his girl, "I love you with both my kidneys."

Or, "Hey, baby, you make my liver quiver."

It's just not the same, is it?

But it could be worse. In fact, it was. You know what the seat of the emotions was in the Old Testament?

The bowels.

I'm not kidding. Look it up.

Boy, that would ruin a lot of good love songs, wouldn't it?

"Don't tell my bowels, my achey-breakey bowels . . ."

"I left my bowels in San Francisco . . ."

What did those Old Testament people DO for love songs?

Think about it. Exchange "heart" for "bowels," and something BIG is lost in the translation. Picture an Old Testament guy putting his arm around his Old Testament girl and whispering, "Oh, baby, oh, baby, you MOVE me."

But even some of our uses for *heart* don't make much sense. Take our Christian cliché: "Would you like to invite Jesus into your heart?"

> I mean it with all my heart, kidneys, liver, and bowels.

Let me tell you something. Jesus is just about as interested in getting into your heart as he is into your kidneys. He doesn't want to get into your left ventricle to watch blood go by.

We know what letting "Jesus into our hearts" means (although I bet American missionaries in liver or kidney countries get some good laughs with it.)

But do we know what it really means?

When you invite Jesus into your "heart," get ready. At times, you may have a broken heart.

A lot of Christians believe that coming to Jesus will make everything fine forever.

Christ said he came to give us "life."

But not just life—life more "abundant."

And, first, before you can have an *abundant* amount of life, you've got to have the normal amount of life.

You know what life is? Whether you're a believer or not

161

a believer, life is life. Life is a series of emotions. Life is a mountain after a valley, a wife to feed, a husband to clothe, children to raise, a boss to put up with, car payments, taxes, April 15.

LIFE is LIFE.

And Christ said, "I've come to give you life more abundant." He came to give us . . . a lot of it!

That almost sounds like a warning.

If I could describe the Christian life in one word, know what it would be? It wouldn't be *joyous*, it wouldn't be *victorious*, it wouldn't be *sad*, it wouldn't be *depressing*, even though it has been all those things at some point in time. If I could put my entire Christian experience into one word, it would be: *interesting*.

You want a boring life? Don't come to Christ. You want an interesting life, come to Christ.

Heart, liver, kidney, bowels. All of them are in for a ride.

Here's a scripture for you.

This is my favorite—my life-verse.

Ready? Here it comes:

"And it came to pass."

I love that phrase. It didn't come to stay, it came to pass. No matter where you are on your journey, it will pass.

Got a broken heart?

It will pass.

Got gray hair? Blue hair? No hair? Store-bought hair? (Then your hair's already come to pass, hasn't it? I saw a TV preacher the other day wearing the nastiest-looking wig I've ever seen in my life. I think the thing was made out of cat hair. Every time he scratched his head, his rear went up.)

Whatever it is—enjoy it. It will pass.

You may even have arthritis living in your joints. Hey, enjoy it, because it will pass. Either it will pass, or you will pass.

"It came to pass."

Are you having a bad year? Hold on, it will pass.

Are you having a good year? Hold on, it will pass.

No matter where you are in your life, no matter what you're going through, this, too, shall pass.

And I mean it with all my heart, kidneys, liver, and bowels.

The Plumber's Coming in the Morning

When I first started traveling with an evangelist during college, I didn't have to do much talking. I would stand up, sing, and sit down. Which is what most pastors wish all singers would do. Then, when I went out on my own I had to be interesting while the sound man changed the soundtracks. Those few seconds seemed like an eternity. I think some churches find the oldest person in their church, the one who's hard of hearing and changes the oil on the church buses, to also run the sound. They're never in a hurry changing those tracks.

Trying to talk and at the same time be theologically correct while waiting for the next song to start is a singer's nightmare.

I remember one of the first gospel singers I ever heard. He was nervous, and his speaking voice had a kind of unnatural high pitch to it, a little breathy, as if saying to the audience, "I really mean this from my heart."

Just before he sang, he said, "God has given me this song."

Then I heard the song.

I thought, "God, why would you do that?"

It would have made Fanny Crosby do backflips in her grave.

You know what I mean. You've heard 'em, too.

I decided I was going to be different. I would just be me, which is different enough. This ol' gospel singer was really gonna get his act together. Since I went to a good Bible college, I knew being theologically correct would be no problem. So I started talking about my family, growing up in Texas, being sent to a psychiatrist in the third grade, quoting letters I wrote to my sixth-grade teacher that got me a three-day vacation from school. And people seemed to enjoy my little monologues between songs. Actually, I think they enjoyed them more than my singing, which was all right with me. And since my calendar has stayed full, I figured I'd just keep talking. And I'm still doing it.

But you know, God's also got a sense of humor.

One day, after spraying my apartment, a Pentecostal-ish exterminator tried for an hour to convince me that I needed to be rebaptized. I handled him pretty well. That Bible-college degree was coming in handy.

Then the next day I had to call a locksmith. After I handed him my check, he asked me what I thought about the kingdom of God. I said I was all for it. I asked him what church he was with. He said he was a Jehovah's Witness.

At that point, I said, with great confidence, "The main

difference you and I have theologically is that you don't believe Jesus was God."

The man said, "No, he wasn't. He was the son of God."

"That's true," I answered. "He was the son of God. But He was also God on foot. Christ said (and here I added my preacher-voice for emphasis), 'Anyone who has seen me, has seen the Father.' And that 'He thought it not robbery to be equal with God. And that "in Him dwells all the fullness of the Godhead bodily."' That sort of Scripture stuff. Then, as my finale, I quoted him John 1:1: "In the beginning was the Word, and the Word was with God, and the Word was God . . ."

Of course, I had to stop and look it up to quote it correctly. And after I did, he proceeded to quote the rest of the chapter from memory. Plus most of the New Testament, Proverbs, and ALL of Revelation.

I felt smaller and smaller and smaller as the guy spouted and spouted and spouted. I was embarrassed I didn't know my Bible better.

But give me a break, I wanted to say! I'm a gospel singer!

I finally ended our conversation by telling him that I had trusted Jesus as my Lord, Savior, and God. So no problems, and bye-bye now.

The Holy Spirit started convicting me before the unsaved locksmith had closed the door to my apartment. "Mark," he said, "you have the truth in your heart, but what you need is the Word."

There's really no excuse. I will be studying the Word more. I will be prepared next time.

Do me a favor, though. Keep me in your prayers—the plumber's coming in the morning.

Life Backwards

I have a perfect older brother, as I've mentioned. And he married a perfect woman, and they've given birth to four perfect children. Christopher Michael Lowry, Courtney Gail Lowry, Chad Alan Lowry—Alan, named after me, Mark Alan—and the newest and last (thanks to modern surgery and much to my brother's chagrin), Chelsea Nicole.

Chad looks like me. Poor child. His head is my size. I have always had a head like a large cantaloupe. I kind of grew into it. If I had been a little taller, it would have fit.

Being born with a head bigger than a melon caused a lot of self-image problems when I was a little kid, because other kids would make fun of my having a little-bitty body and this huge head. I'd come home from school and say, "Mama, everybody's making fun of my head again."

She'd say, "Oh, Mark, it's okay," while she rubbed my head very similarly to the way she polished the coffee table.

But Chad, he's a cutie. He'll grow into his head, too.

Christopher, though, was the firstborn. The firstborn gets all the home movies, all the snapshots, all the Polaroids, all the videos.

The second one gets a couple of snapshots.

The last one is lucky to get her footprints on her birth certificate.

When I first went to meet Christopher Michael Lowry, I rocked him all day long. (I used small rocks; it didn't hurt bad.)

He was a fat baby. I like fat babies. I don't like skinny babies. Skinny babies make me nervous. They look like they'd break if you dropped them. If you dropped fat babies, they'd just bounce back.

I was rocking Christopher back and forth, back and forth, back and forth, talking to him. He fell asleep in my arms. (Rocking tip: The tighter you squeeze a baby when you're rocking them, the quicker it goes to sleep. I think it has to do something with a lack of oxygen getting to its brain.) It was the first time I had ever had a baby sleep in my arms. He was a cute little thing. His mouth fell open, and he didn't have a tooth in his head.

"Christopher, this is your Uncle Mark talking. You don't know me yet, but we're going to be friends," I said. "Christopher, you are a fortunate child. You have a mommy and a daddy who both love you. Did you know that?"

He just lay there.

"Christopher, did you know you have a mommy and a daddy who not only love you, they love each other? You're a fortunate kid, and you don't seem to appreciate it.

"Christopher, did you know that not only do your mommy and daddy love you and love each other, but they love Jesus? Did you know that? Well, you don't seem to appreciate it.

"Christopher, did you know that you live in America?

You weren't born in Ethiopia or Bangladesh, Christopher. You were born in America, the land of the free and the home of the brave. It's time you appreciated it.

"Christopher, did you know you don't have to mow the grass? You don't have to pay the bills. You don't have to pay the mortgage or the car note. You have no tests to pass . . . April 15 means nothing to you. And you don't seem to appreciate it."

By that point, I was getting pretty ticked.

It wasn't fair to have it made and not appreciate it.

So I came to the conclusion, rocking Christopher, that the life cycle is backward.

I think it should be like this. We should die first and get that out of the way. Then we immediately go to a nursing home, until they kick us out because we're too young. Then we get a gold watch, go to work, and work for forty years until we're young enough to enjoy our retirement. Then we graduate and go to college. Then we graduate and go to high school. Then we don't worry about college or high school, because we've already graduated.

Then we become a little kid, we play, have no responsibilities, and we appreciate it!

We spend our last nine months floating, playing underwater jump rope, and end up a gleam in our daddy's eye.

Wouldn't that be great?

Well Worshiping

When I was growing up in Texas, I thought there was only one kind of Christian.

My kind.

I was raised in an independent, fundamentalist, Bible-believin', Bible-bangin', foot-stompin', door-knockin', soul-winnin', devil-chasin', sin-hatin', pew-jumpin', hand-raisin', King-James-only Baptist church.

I was born again in that church, and I naturally assumed if you weren't part of that church, your chances of making it to heaven were about as good as Ross Perot's chances of finding earmuffs that fit.

When I first began my ministry, I only traveled to Baptist churches. That's who I knew, and that's who knew me. Then I started receiving invitations from other churches. I've performed concerts for the Methodist, Presbyterian, Charismatic, Charismatic-Catholic, Church of God-Cleveland, the Church of God-Anderson, Lutheran, Seventh-Day Adventist, Christian Church, Evangelical Free, Grace Brethren, Southern Baptist, Northern Baptist, Free-Will Baptist, Hard-Shell Baptist, General Association of Regular Baptists, General Association of Irregular Baptists, Conservative Baptist, Moderate Baptist, Liberal Baptist, and a host of other churches I can't remember at this particular moment in time. (Whew, that gave me a headache!)

One Baptist pastor told me that if he ever heard I was singing in anything but a Baptist church, he'd never have me back.

169

> Heaven is going to be populated with surprises. I honestly believe that.

"Well, I guess you wouldn't have Jesus because He was never in a Baptist church," I respectfully pointed out. I've never been back to that haven of hospitality.

Heaven is going to be populated with surprises. I honestly believe that. Not only are we going to see people we were absolutely sure were not going to make it, they might even have bigger mansions than ours. And some of the ones we counted on being there for some reason are going to be "no shows."

I believe there are true Christians in every denomination, in every city, in every state, and in every country in the world. Like Jesus put it in John 10:16, "I have sheep that are not of this fold . . ."

Originally, there was only one church, of course. It began at Pentecost, and from there it started splitting, reproducing, multiplying. Every time someone tried to stick God in a box to figure him out, in order to franchise the formula, he moved on. That's how he works. Just when we think we know who he uses and who he loves, he blows our mind by using someone we wouldn't be seen with and loving someone we can't stand.

Even Jesus was full of surprises. He hung out with people the pious religious crowd thought were bad influences. He was a friend of sinners, tax collectors, murderers, and thieves. He showed love to the cheats, the scoundrels, the drunkards, and the prostitutes.

The only people Jesus ever chewed out were the religious folk, those pious gasbags who were polished on the outside but full of dead men's bones on the inside.

Ever notice that? Jesus never had an unkind word for sinners, but he went out of his way to put the Pharisees and Sadducees in their places.

I have evidence.

Here's his response to the woman taken in adultery: "Neither do I condemn thee: go, and sin no more."

Pretty lenient, nonjudgmental stuff, right?

Here's his good word for Pharisees: "You're of your father the devil and the lust of your father you will do."

Pretty tough stuff, right?

I honestly don't believe it matters whether you jump pews or sleep in them. The Pharisees did everything "right" except what mattered. They talked of God but didn't recognize him when they saw him.

Don't misunderstand me. I'm not against the church. I love it. I just don't believe we can confine God to any denomination or limit him by boundaries we try to impose. He's the God of us all, and he can be found wherever there is a need.

So you can't judge a church by how loud they shout, how big their building is, or how many people attend. They may be serving up waste instead of Water.

We should observe, instead, how many orphans they clothe and how many widows they feed.

We should be able to hear the truth about the church in the pastor's sermon.

Is the message fuller of what the pastor has done for God than what God's done for the pastor? Does it lift up the church's accomplishments more than Jesus'?

If it does, watch out.

Let's face it, some churches are deader than the desert. Once they were full of Living Water, wells overflowing with truth and life.

But the well ran dry.

It could be because the guy dipping into the well became more enamored with the well than the Water.

Maybe he started telling the thirsty they couldn't have any Water unless they wore the right kind of clothes, made the right kind of donation, carried the right kind of Bible, or performed the right kind of job around the well.

So the Water, being a Living Entity, flowed on to another well, and those around the old well didn't even notice when the dipper came up empty.

Oh, it's still a beautiful well, with its bricks and stained glass, but take heed.

You'll dehydrate and die if you fall in love with the well and not the Water.

Relatively Perfect

The other day while eating lunch with my older brother, Mike, I came up with the idea to write a routine about what it must have been like to be one of Jesus' younger siblings. How would it have felt to have a perfect older brother? Mike pointed out that I shouldn't have any problem relating to that.

But think about it.

Imagine what it must have been like to be one of Jesus' brothers or sisters.

Life around Joseph and Mary's household must have been pretty hard with Jesus for an older brother.

For one thing, it's probably safe to say that Baby Jesus hardly ever cried. He knew that in whatsoever state he was, therewith to be content. He didn't throw tantrums or dump his oatmeal on his head. He was no doubt the perfect baby.

He surely didn't go through the "terrible twos." While other two-year-olds were acting like miniature battering rams in diapers, destroying everything in their path, Jesus was sitting quietly in his chair, trying to remember why he ever bothered to create such rowdy two-year-olds. He obeyed his parents, never stayed up past his bedtime, or screamed "Mine! Mine! Mine!" while playing with a neighbor's toy. He had to be a parent's dream.

As a matter of fact, Mary and Joseph probably had such an easy time raising Jesus that they later decided to have children of their own.

And that's where the trouble surely kicked in. As long as Mary stayed with just the immaculately conceived baby, childrearing was a breeze. But as soon as Joseph started fathering their offspring, there was trouble right there in Nazareth city.

Think what Jesus' brothers and sisters must have heard from their mother every day:

"Why don't you act like your older brother?"

"Jesus never talks back."

"Jesus never leaves his robe and sandals lying around the house."

"Jesus doesn't have to be reminded to do his homework."

It had to have been tough—so tough that I've been told Jesus' siblings weren't believers until after his resurrection. They had a hard time acknowledging that their older brother was the Creator of the universe.

My brother and I couldn't even agree which one of us was going to reign over the television remote.

That's because my brother, however perfect he seems to me, isn't Jesus, and was born with the same sinful nature as mine.

I may not have had Mary suggesting to me that I should be more like Jesus. But every once in a while, in much gentler tones than even a mother could utter, the Spirit of God has said, "Hey, Mark, cut it out!"

A Fate Worse Than Death

Someone once said that for a man to know what childbirth feels like he must pull his top lip over his head.

God has a better sense of humor than that.

And I know this because I read the Bible.

I love Bible stories. Jonah and the whale, Noah and the ark, Jezebel and the dogs. Zacchaeus up a tree.

But there's one story that's a doozy.

It's the story of Job.

Job was a good man. He was a righteous man. He didn't cheat on his taxes. He didn't cheat on his wife. He took good care of his children. He was honored in his city. His employees thought he was just wonderful. Everybody respected Job because he had earned it.

Life was good.

Then one day Satan was in heaven making his report to God. Even Satan has to report to God. God asked him where he'd been.

Satan said, "I've been roaming on the earth, doing my thing."

Then God said, "Have you considered my servant Job?"

Get that. God himself brought Job to Satan's attention.

Satan said, "No, as a matter of fact, I haven't. You've built a hedge around him. And I bet if you remove that hedge, he'll curse you."

Well, you know the story. God removed the hedge he'd placed around Job and allowed Satan to wipe out his crops, slay his servants, kill his children, plunder his riches, attack his health, and defame his character.

I've often wondered why God didn't make the devil take Job's wife while he was at it. That seemed like the least God could've done for Job.

Why? Because, it seems to me Job's wife was on Satan's side. After Job had lost everything but his wife—Satan wasn't about to kill her; she was his best offense—she said to Job, "Why don't you curse God and die?"

There you have it. The mouth of a critic. Ever notice there are no monuments raised to critics?

But his wife paid dearly for giving that advice. Serving Satan always costs more than it pays. Because at the end of the story God replaced everything to Job TWOFOLD!

God replaced his livestock.

Gave him new servants.

Restored his health.

Allowed him to grow some more crops.

And made him twice as rich as before, his reputation greater than ever.

And then God gave Job a new crop of kids.

Think about it. That poor woman had a fate worse than death. She had to go through the pain of delivering TEN MORE KIDS!

And I bet through every last pang of all ten deliveries, she was wishing she'd never opened her mouth with that stupid advice. **✗**

She should've just pulled her top lip over her head instead. It would've been a lot less painful.

Takin' Time to Be Thankful

Not too long ago, the Brooklyn Tabernacle Choir invited the Vocal Band to sing at Radio City Music Hall in New York City.

What a great honor it was to sing in such a great and historic theater.

New York is a fast-paced city. It's nice to visit, but I wouldn't want to live in such a hectic place. You have to

✗ A bore is someone who stubbornly holds onto his own views after I've enlightened him with mine.

have a special kind of temperament to live there. It's sort of like being a flea on an overcrowded dog.

Our hotel was a few blocks down from Radio City, so every evening, we walked to the hall for the concerts.

The hall was sold out every night.

We found out why. It wasn't because we were so incredibly popular. Brooklyn Tabernacle had given away many of the tickets to the homeless.

After the concerts each night, I walked back to my hotel. Every night I saw the same thing on the way. A little lady about fifty-five years old was sleeping on a marble slab in front of a downtown bank. She wore a coat, a little cap, red socks, and brown shoes. And when I passed her after the concerts, she was always sound asleep.

I wondered how she got there—where she came from.

How do you get to the place where you have no place to sleep? No place to call home?

Here was a lady who at one time was somebody's little girl. Maybe somebody's bride and wife. Maybe somebody's mother.

But now she was all alone in an overcrowded city.

Is it just as hard to make it to the bottom as it is to the top?

Sometimes I feel sorry for myself. I feel like a dog chasing his tail, always reaching for the goal yet always missing it by just a few inches. When I pay my mortgage, there's always next month to pay. When I pay my car payment, there's still next month's that will show up in the mail. When I pay the gas, electric, water, garbage pickup, tuition, pension plan, taxes, there's always next month's, next year's to pay.

To realize the bills never end is disheartening.

Disheartening, that is, until you pass that little lady on the marble slab with the red socks. She doesn't have a house or a car, or a gas, electricity, or water bill to pay. She doesn't have clean sheets to slide between each night. She doesn't have an air conditioner to cool her down in the summertime or a heater to turn up in the winter. I'm sure she'd love to have a hot shower and a home-cooked meal. But somehow she's lost all of that.

A few days after going home, I was eating at Morrison's Cafeteria. I had fried chicken, broccoli with cheese, jalapeño cornbread, and iced tea. I was looking at that chicken and thinking, "This bird didn't die in vain, because I'm about to enjoy his sacrifice."

Most days I pray before I eat. I was trained to do that. When I was a kid, we always bowed our heads and thanked the Lord for our food. It's a habit and a good one. But sometimes it's more tradition than sincerity.

That day in Morrison's, before I dove into that good lunch, I thought again about that lady on the marble slab.

I said, "Lord, I'm really thankful for this food; you've been so good to me. You've given me bills to pay and money to pay them.

"Lord, bless this food and bless that lady wherever she is tonight."

Since I've Given Up Hope

I hardly ever drive to my concerts anymore. As I've said, I fly everywhere. If it's across town and there's a flight, I take it. But for some reason, one weekend I got an urge to drive.

I'm a strange musician.

I never listen to music on the radio. Music will put me into a coma quicker than just about anything, and that's not healthy when you're driving. So I listen to talk radio.

I love talk radio. I listen to it all the time. I especially like it when the hosts are rude, getting into arguments and cutting off callers. My favorite talk-show hosts are psychologists who give stupid advice.

But driving home from Austin, I lost all contact with my favorite talk-radio stations. So there I was, scanning the stations looking for a good debate, a woman preacher, anything that would keep me awake.

All I could find, though, were country music stations.

And I made a great discovery. Even talk radio won't keep you awake like the twang of a country radio station.

So I tuned in to the clearest channel of country music and started to listen.

Being a lyricist myself, I listen to the words. And I heard some of the most depressing words I've ever heard.

You know the kind:

"Let's Fall to Pieces Together"

"80 Proof Bottle or Tear Stopper"

"Making the Best of a Bad Situation"

"Whiskey River"

"Ruby, Don't Take Your Love to Town"

"One-Night Stands"
"How's My Ex Treatin' You?"
"He's Breathin' Down My Neck"
"If Drinkin' Don't Kill Me Her Memory Will"
"I Put a Golden Band on the Right Left Hand This Time"

—and the funniest title of the day:

"Don't Leave without Taking Your Silver"

The one thing that stood out in my mind while listening to all those country songs is that they were so hopeless. All the people were just wandering from bedroom to bedroom and bottle to bottle.

Oh, I heard a few uplifting ones that day, like "God Bless the USA," but they were few and miles between.

What do we have if we don't have hope?

Nothing.

You may say, "But Mark, I'm poor, my wife just died, I lost my job, I'm failing all my classes, I have thirteen terminal diseases, and I don't have a thing to wear."

There's still hope.

"Our present sufferings are not worth comparing to the glory that will be revealed to us . . ."

"We know that the whole creation has been groaning as in the pains of childbirth right up to the present time. Not only so, but we ourselves who have the firstfruits of the Spirit, groan inwardly as we wait eagerly for our adoption as sons, the redemption of our bodies. For in this hope we were saved.

"Hope that is seen is no hope at all. Who hopes for what he already has? But if we hope for what we don't yet have, we wait for it patiently."

Sound familiar? It came straight out of the mouth of the apostle Paul, who obviously knew something about hope. And about the source of our hope.

We've got hope.

The best hope of all.

Jesus is our hope. Children of God, wait eagerly and have hope. You may be poor, but have hope. Jesus is preparing a mansion for you. Your wife may have died, but have hope; you'll see her again some day. You may have lost your job, but have hope. I've never seen the righteous forsaken or their seed begging for bread. You may have thirteen terminal diseases, but have hope and wait eagerly for the redemption of your body. You may not have a thing to wear, but have hope. He's promised us a robe of righteousness and a crown of life.

Have hope, as Paul told Titus, while "we wait for the blessed hope—the glorious appearing of our great God and Savior, Jesus Christ."

SINCE HOPE WON'T GIVE UP ON ME, I GOTTA FEEL BETTER.

Shrimp Nightmares

Ever had a nightmare? I mean a real nightmare?
How about one that you were AWAKE through?
Oooh.

One night I talked late into the night to my producer at Word Records about some very important decisions I had to make. By the time I got through with that conversation around midnight I was wide awake, too wired to go to sleep. But it was late, so I went to bed.

I had already taken some cough syrup with codeine that the doctor had given me for a case of bronchitis I was fighting. But I was still wide-eyed and bushy-tailed. So I made a bad medicine-cabinet decision.

Tip for the pharmaceutically challenged: Do not take Tylenol PM after you've taken codeine cough syrup. These two are NOT A HAPPY COMBINATION.

I fell asleep all right, but at 5:55 in the morning I awoke.

Startled awake. Shaken awake.

Scared out of my mind.

I was lying there with my eyes wide open staring at the darkness, one ear in the pillow and one facing the ceiling.

Because I heard things.

When one ear is covered and the other is exposed, your hearing perception is off. And what I heard was growling noises.

Then I heard what sounded like thumping footsteps. It sounded like some sulfur-snorting demon.

I was afraid to move, afraid what I was hearing was in the room. Afraid that the thing I couldn't see in the dark had night vision and was gleefully staring at me from the foot of the bed.

That made me move ever so slowly toward the middle of the bed. I turned over, exposing the ear that had been buried in the pillow and burying the other one at the exact same time.

And again I heard the sounds—a creaking, gurgling, and bubbling inferno.

Finally, I bolted straight up in the bed, flipped on the nightstand light, and listened with both ears.

And guess what.

That sulfur-snorting demon was my stomach! I had eaten some fried shrimp with fried onion rings, and my stomach was trying to digest that bowl of grease. And hearing that with only one ear at a time sounded like something coming up from the charred pits of hell.

I'll be honest. I pray a lot when I'm scared. I almost become a Bapticostal. I rebuke the devil, claim the Blood, renounce the powers of darkness. I tend to forget my practical, intellectual, "theologically correct" upbringing and lean more toward my pew-walking, tongue-talking, devil-chasing friends.

At least I have Someone to call on when I'm scared. What do atheists do? Who does someone like Madalyn Murray O'Hair call on when she's frightened in the night? Who holds her hand when it feels like hell is holding her? Who speaks peace to her world when her world is falling to pieces?

I'm thankful for the promises of a better world to come. I'm excited about living in a land where the lamb lies down with the lion and the night never comes. But, hey, I'm not there yet. Right now, I'm more excited that when I'm scared, I have Someone bigger than me to call on.

So for the sake of Madalyn Murray O'Hair and the other atheists out there, I suggest they stay away from greasy shrimp.

But my stomach-gurgling waking nightmare made me aware of other things about the nighttime, about the power that the DARK has on us.

On another night, I woke up convinced there was a real boogieman nearby. (And this time it wasn't from eating shrimp.)

It was 3:57 A.M. I was awakened from a deep sleep by a frightening sound . . . like someone was walking through my apartment. I couldn't see anything because my room is so dark that at high noon, if it weren't for my alarm clock, I wouldn't know it was daylight.

I woke from dreamland into a very scary, dark place.

So what's the first reaction of a man of steel?

I wouldn't know, but my reaction was clever.

I pulled the sheets up around my neck. Everyone knows bullets can't pierce sheets. I was sure that any second I would feel the cold, piercing slice from the intruder's hunting knife or hear the whooshing sound of bullets flying from the barrel of a gun with a silencer.

"WHAT SHOULD I DO?" I kept thinking, quivering under my sheet.

"If I dial 911, will the police arrive before the burglar steals my genuine imitation leather jacket I left lying on the couch? Or my computer on which I store all these nuggets of wisdom you're paying good money for?

"Or what about my genuine, fake, brand-new antique Tiffany lamp I bought in New York City?"

As my heart was racing like the sound of a hummingbird's wings I decided:

"NO!!

"I'll get out from under these warm covers, turn on the lights, and face the intruder head-on!"

I edged out from under my sheet, I tiptoed to the lightswitch, I poised to bop the armed intruder over the head with my pillow-soft fist, AND . . .

> God does that sometimes . . . turns the lights out so we can hear better.

Guess what.

This time, the boogieman was just a straining icemaker trying its best to dispose of some old ice.

I had a hard time getting back to sleep that night. I admit that. I had learned that, in some ways, I'm still scared of the dark.

But this is what I've learned from my experience.

You can hear in the dark.

You can't always feel what you hear. You can't always taste what you hear. You can't always smell what you hear. And you can never see what you hear.

But you CAN hear what you hear.

And, oh, what you hear in the dark that you never hear in the daytime! You hear things you'd never hear during the day while the kids are screaming, the television's blaring, and the radio's singing.

Alone in a house at 3:57 in the morning, your imagination runs wild. You can hear a house settle, a mouse chewing, a refrigerator running, your stomach digesting grease.

You'll hear the house settle and think it's a ghost.

You'll hear a neighbor in the next apartment walking to his bathroom, and you'll think he's walking to yours.

You'll hear an icemaker groan and see your life flash before your eyes.

God does that sometimes . . . turns the lights out so we can hear better.

It's amazing how well we listen when the lights are out. And when God turns out the light, it's DARK. You won't be able to see, but you can still hear—hear a still, small voice that will lead you back into the Light.

When people tell me they've seen Jesus, I always wonder if they had too much pizza the night before.

I believe you can hear Jesus, though. I have.

He didn't say, "My sheep know my face" or "see my hand." Jesus said, "My sheep hear my voice." It's really easy to hear him in the dark.

Are You Lonely Tonight?

I ate with some friends several years ago at a Japanese steakhouse—one of those restaurants where a bunch of strangers sit around a table/grill together and a Japanese cook with a tall, white hat throws your uncooked dinner around in the air while you watch.

My friends are married—nineteen years and counting. They have two children, a teenage daughter and a six-year-old surprise son named Richard.

My friend Rick started telling me about how he's really had to bone up on algebra to understand his fifteen-year-old's algebra problems. He thought he'd never have to go through that again. He told me about her boyfriends, the ones he liked and the one with the tattoos (which is the one *she* likes). Then he spent the next fifteen minutes telling me about his son's innate gift for writing and how "he's also really the little athlete."

While I was sitting there listening to this parade of

events in the life of a happy family, the flow of conversation drifted toward me.

"So, what did you do today, Mark?"

I told them about working on my computer, doing the laundry, taking a nap on the couch during *A Current Affair*, and basically doing nothing for the rest of the day. They gave me one of those "how nice" smiles. Then they asked the question. They both did it together. A duet. It sounded like the Judds:

"So, when are you getting married?"

I told them I had to get married this year. I was thirty-three, and the Lord laid down his life when he was thirty-three.

They didn't laugh. They looked at each other, trying their best to show me how happy they were, smiling that sappy, sweet, gooey smile that married people sometimes muster. Then they turned back to me with the most pitiful looks still on their faces.

I thought they had a pair of blowfish stuck in their throats.

My married friends want me married. All of them. They try to make it sound like they're worried about me being lonely. (It sounds to me like misery loves company.) They worry about me not having any kids. They think I'd make a good father. (I think I'd make a terrible father. I can see it now. My fifteen-year-old daughter comes home from school with algebra problems, and I have to admit, "Sorry, honey, Daddy can't help you with algebra 'cause he never learned his times tables.")

Rick asked me in front of all those strangers and that Japanese cook (who was busy throwing knives over my head and shooting flames through my hair), "Don't you ever get lonely?"

"Yeah," I said, "don't you?"

He gulped, looked straight ahead; his wife's eyes went to her plate.

A cool breeze suddenly swept through the room (which was fortunate because it put out the fire in my hair).

Everybody gets lonely. And there's nothing wrong with it.

Jesus got lonely. Says so right in the book of Mark: "Jesus could no longer enter a town openly but stayed outside in lonely places." Because of the news of Christ's healing power he had to get away, become a recluse. He had to be alone. And the Bible calls where he went, "lonely places."

All of us have a lonely place inside our hearts. And being around other people, including our own families, can't change that. Some of the loneliest people I've ever seen are in America's cities. They're surrounded by millions of people, but they're walking around in their own, private, personal lonely places.

The simple fact is this: We're not in Eden anymore. We've been kicked out. No one got to stay. Married, single, divorced, widowed, orphaned . . . everybody out. Evicted. And we've been lonely ever since.

Lonely for Eden.

Getting saved assures us that God is with us, but at times we're still lonely.

Why?

Because this ain't home. We're not supposed to stay here.

We're from Eden. We'll never be totally happy until we're back in perfect fellowship with God again.

But until then, we'll just have to go through some lonely places.

The Bible says it best—we're waiting like a bride waiting on her bridegroom.

At times you may feel like He's taking His own sweet time about it. But that's okay. Just remember you're not alone. He's paid too much for you to give up on you now. He may be silent. You may not feel His touch. But as Gloria Gaither says, "He's up to something. It is eternal. And it is for your good."

Alarm-Clock Faith

I like feelings. I like goose bumps. When Sandi Patty sings, sometimes my goose bumps give birth to goose bumps.

But I tell you what, it's scary to base your whole salvation on goose bumps. I did that for the first few years of my life. When I was a medium-size kid, Mama used to sit me on a chair and have me sing in our home church. And I'd get these goosebumps up and down my spine when I'd sing a song called "The King Is Coming."

I used to think, "Ah, I must be saved. I got a chill."

I found out you can get the flu and get a chill.

And if you've got to feel saved to know you are saved, you're not going to be saved most of the time. Because salvation is something that runs deeper than our emotions.

On June 5, 1973, I got saved, and there have been many days since that I have not felt saved.

Example: Not too long ago, I had to get up at 4:30 in the morning. I didn't know 4:30 came twice a day. I don't like mornings. I figure if the Lord wanted me to see the sunrise, He'd put it in the middle of the day.

I don't know what you're doing at 4:30 in the morning, but I was in a coma. I was visiting the sandman. I was sleeping, sawing logs, and having a good time. I had to get up for some particular reason. I don't remember what it was. But I set my alarm clock for 4:30.

I don't have a pretty alarm clock. My older brother has a pretty alarm clock—a woman's alarm clock. It has a little AM radio on top, an FM radio underneath, and, down at the opposite end, it has these BIG red numbers that blare out into the darkness.

Helen Keller could see this clock.

With my brother's clock, you don't have to pop in your contacts, you don't have to find your glasses, you don't have to flip on the light. There it is, 4:30! No mistaking that.

But have you heard those pretty clocks go off? Say it's 4:30 in the morning, and my brother's clock goes off.

It sounds like this: mmmmmmmmm . . .

That wouldn't pull me out of a daydream.

But I've got a MAN'S alarm clock. It's one of those boxy kind. It used to have a face, but I knocked that off a long time ago.

And when it goes off, it doesn't go mmmmmmmmm.

It goes AAAHHHNNNNNNNNNNNNNNNHH!!

That thing went off at 4:30 in the morning, right in the middle of my deepest dreaming. My right foot was telling my left foot, "I got out of bed first last time. It's your turn." My left foot said, "But I'm paralyzed."

I told them both to shut up; I was trying to sleep.

Finally I crawled out of my bed, and I stumbled into the darkness because even the sun has better sense than to be up at 4:30.

And I've got to tell you, at that moment I put the death grip on that alarm clock. I did NOT feel saved. I did not LOOK saved. And I certainly did not SMELL saved. I felt lost. But if the Lord comes back at 4:30 in the morning, I'm going.

I may be there two hours before I realize what happened, but I'm going.

Actually, the Lord IS coming back between four and five in the morning. Want to know how I know? Somewhere on this planet, it's always between four and five in the morning, so he's going to wake some "body" up. I just hope it's YOUR body and not mine.

But if the Lord comes back at 4:30 in the morning, I'm going. I may not feel like going, but I'm going.

I am not depending on how I feel.

And that sure makes me feel a whole lot better.

Can't Fail

Pretend, for just a moment, that for the rest of your life you had one thing different about you.

Your face wouldn't change; your personality wouldn't change; your financial position wouldn't change.

You wouldn't have to change your spouse, your kids, your job, or the school you go to.

You wouldn't even have to change your church.

The one thing that would be different about you is this: From now on YOU COULDN'T FAIL.

What would you do?

How would that change your life? What would you do differently that you're not doing now?

If I knew I couldn't fail, I would sit down to write songs that would praise the Lord the way no human tongue has ever thought to praise Him.

I would start writing new humorous material for my concerts, and all of it would be GREAT.

I would start taking voice lessons and singing notes no human has ever performed. I'd make Pavarotti sound like he should be singing bass for the Blackwood Brothers.

I'd have a concert program that ran so smooth, it'd make Bill Gaither look like a beginner.

I'd have enough platform charisma to make Carman look like he's never stood before an audience before.

And yet I would be able, with the flicker of an eye, to change from sidesplitting humor to heart-gripping, mind-provoking, tear-jerking seriousness that would make Gloria Gaither look like she was only kidding.

I'd have the looks of a young Robert Redford (after paying for the plastic surgery that couldn't fail with the money from the royalties those big "Praise Hits" brought me).

I'd have an office building bigger than Billy Graham's with my name emblazoned on the side of it: MARK LOWRY "NEVER CAN FAIL" MINISTRIES, Inc.

I'd have a TV show that . . .

Well, you get the idea.

Maybe that's why we're not supposed to be great at everything—maybe we're suppose to fail.

Maybe we wouldn't succeed at anything if we were great at everything.

Maybe that's how the body of Christ is supposed to be a "body" with different parts. All the different parts doing what they do best, leaving the feet to walk, the mouth to talk, and the forefinger to scratch what itches.

And for a forefinger to be the best at scratching what itches, which is what it was created to do, a forefinger surely can't be going around trying to walk or talk, because it would fail miserably, wouldn't it?

Looking Forward

 I've spent most of my life looking forward. I look forward to Thanksgiving (in spite of football), when I'm home with my family sitting around my mother's 5'x16' dining-room table, eating that bountiful feast. (She can seat about sixteen people at that table, and every Thanksgiving it's usually full. You've got to make reservations a year in advance, even if you're one of her kids.)

I look forward to Christmas when all the presents are passed out.

I look forward to my birthday. Well, I used to. I'm starting to actually dread it because it comes too often. It used to mosey around once a year, but now it seems to come every six months.

I usually have more fun looking forward to something than actually doing it.

I spend two months looking forward to Thanksgiving, and then the turkey may be dry, and someone has the AUDACITY to make bread dressing instead of cornbread dressing! I start looking forward to Christmas shopping the day following Thanksgiving and spend a lot of time buying presents and having them wrapped. Then, with a flick of the wrist, the wrapping paper falls to the floor, and the recipients scream, "Oh, my, it's just what we WANTED!" Then they take them back the following day to get what they *really* wanted.

And it's the day AFTER Christmas.

Again.

Looking forward to things is great.

But the memories can be greater.

My grandfather spent the last two years of his life in a nursing home. He had a stroke. He was the greatest Paw Paw a kid could have. But Paw Paw couldn't remember very well toward the end. Mama would visit him in the morning, and when she'd come back that afternoon, he couldn't remember that she'd been there that morning.

But Paw Paw could remember yesteryear. He remembered working for Humble Oil Company, which is now Exxon. He remembered working for a sheet-metal company in Houston. He could remember the church's Sunday dinners on the ground and his years singing in the male quartet.

But the last years of his life he just sat in his wheelchair looking forward to the Lord coming back. He looked forward to a day when memories and plans are one and the same. There's no night there, and time is a thing of the past. And I'm sure, over the door of heaven there must be a sign that reads: NO WHEELCHAIRS, HOSPITAL BEDS, OR BEDPANS ALLOWED!

It doesn't take much to excite me. I look forward to getting new things,—new clothes, a new car, a new home. But those days were over for Paw Paw. He had many reasons to look forward to heaven. His wheelchair will not be needed, his hospital bed will be history, and his mind will be brand-new.

He looked forward to going "home." And I'd rarely see him without a smile on his face, because he knew where he was going.

I've always said there's no fear in graduating from high school if you know where you're going. There's no fear in graduating from college if you know where you're going. So I guess there's no fear in dying if you know where you're going.

I've seen it in Paw Paw's eyes. I've seen it in his smile. He knew where he was going.

Because there was one memory he never forgot: the day the preacher came by his house at 911 Prince Drive in Houston and led him to Christ.

The best way to become Paw Paw's age and have wonderful memories is to live a life with heaven in mind, to always know where you're going.

Let's All Be Heels

"How can I know God's will for my life?"

I've been asked that question countless times by young people with eager eyes, acned complexions, and willing hearts.

They'll also say they would like to do what I do.

I always tell them if they can do ANYTHING else—do it.

Just because performing may look glamorous from an auditorium seat doesn't mean it's an easy life.

YET at the same time, I can say I'd rather be doing this than anything else in the world.

I don't believe God plays games with us. I believe He wants us to know His will more than we could ever desire to know it.

Mind if I quote a little scripture? I can't help myself.

"Be joyful always; pray continually; give thanks in all circumstances, for this is God's will for you in Christ Jesus."

That's what I Thessalonians 5:16–18 says concerning the will of God. Think about it. Being joyful, praying, giving thanks. Sounds like a good life to me.

Is it for everybody?

Everybody has a part and a place.

Isn't it great that God has a sense of humor? Every time I look in a mirror, I thank him for that.

Having friends who are a few bricks short of a load is great, too. I haven't had a normal friend in my life. All my really close friends are funny and different, seeing life upside down and backward.

My friends Rick and Mick Vigneulle, for instance. Rick and Mick were two of my crazy college buddies and 5'4" identical twins. I used to sneak out of my dorm after curfew, and they would be waiting for me at the bottom of the fire escape. Then we'd go over to their house to spend the night. We didn't get much sleep because we'd stay up all night telling jokes and listening to another friend of ours, Steve, the son of an evangelist, imitate preachers. Rick and Mick are still bizarre and ridiculously funny. They are two godly men. I know their wives would say that's debatable, but God is really using these two crazy guys to reach young people.

God also has room in His family for normal, nine-to-five, average people like my father. Dad is a very good man. He is the most relaxed, unassuming person you'll ever meet. He's always about three inches from a coma. Nothing ever riles him.

It does my heart good to know that God uses all kinds of people. People like my dad, who seem to be the human equivalent of a sedative, who are consistent, calm, and usually found in the corner. And people like Mick and Rick, who are outgoing, vivacious, and a little like Brylcreem . . . a little dab will do ya!

God doesn't look for a certain kind of personality to use. He doesn't look for great talents or gifts. He looks for people who are available.

There's only one kind of person God NEVER uses— someone who's not available.

(And this is where I'm taking you. Can you see it coming?)

Ever hammered a nail into a wall with the heel of your

shoe? Why did you do that? Because your perfectly good hammer was back home in the garage.

And you needed that nail in the wall. Now.

The heel of your shoe was available; the hammer wasn't.

So what would you rather be? A beautiful, unused hammer in the garage or a heel on God's shoe?

ANYONE who is a believer in Christ is in the ministry.

And before you answer, think which one has a sole. (Get it? Okay, Miss Barth, it's not spelled correctly but work with me here.)

ANYONE who is a believer in Christ is in the ministry. Why? Because we all are ministers by definition.

To minister is to serve.

Don't get the word *minister* confused with *star*. Jesus Christ wasn't a Superstar. He was a minister, a servant. He served living water to a woman at a well. He created wine for a wedding. He gave sight to the blind, legs to the lame, and a new mind to the demon possessed. He washed the disciples' dirty feet. He didn't have to wash his disciples' feet. He was always serving and seldom being served.

Got an idea about how you might want to serve? Well, keep it loose and open. Because you never know where your dreams will take you when you allow yourself to be a HEEL.

I can remember the speakers at Beulah Land church camp who would urge us to come forward and give our lives to Christ. I would walk down the aisle, pray, and recommit my life to Jesus. That was fine. I'm glad I did that. But now when I think back, asking anyone to give his or her future to Christ is a lot to ask.

How can you give to God something that is not yours to give?

You can't give God tomorrow. You can't give God the next hour. It's not yours to give. You can't give away something you don't have. We're not promised tomorrow. We're not even promised the rest of the day. All we can give him is this moment. This second. This heartbeat. This present moment.

And YET when you're available, interesting things happen.

A question I'm often asked in interviews is, "Where do you see yourself in five years?"

I always say, "I don't." I've never been one to make long-term goals. I'm aware that goes against every positive-thinking, self-help book on how to succeed.

I try to take one day at a time, making short-term goals and hoping I live to see them come to pass—as I eat Mexican food, do my thing, and wait.

I never dreamed eight years ago I'd be where I am today.

I could never dream that big.

It never crossed my mind that I'd be a member of the Gaither Vocal Band. In fact, it shocked a lot of people when Bill Gaither invited me to join. But they weren't shocked half as much as I was. A lot of people told Bill he was crazy—including me. But it's been going on just fine for over eight years.

And it just keeps on keeping on. I mean, look at THIS.

The last thing I ever thought I'd do is write a book!

So to those who are wanting to be the next contemporary Christian music "star," I say, work hard. Accept where you are at this time. Hone your craft. Take singing lessons. Find a hook. Write catchy tunes with creative lyrics. And maybe, just maybe, you'll make it. Besides, fame and fortune aren't the point anyway, right? In the meantime, serve.

Don't ever limit God with your goals. Just try to follow his will one day at a time, and believe me, someday you too will be surprised about where you'll be.

If you don't think your talent is big enough, join the rest of us who are out there doing it anyway! You can't impress God with your talent. He's the one who gave it to you.

Trying to impress God with your talent is like trying to impress Edison with the light bulb.

HE INVENTED IT.

God is looking for some people who will be a very important thing: AVAILABLE.

Hey. LET'S ALL BE HEELS. ✗

✗ End of the book. Finis. So long. Farewell. Adieu. Until we meet again. That's all, folks. (Except for the Last Word, of course.)

The Last Word

Like I've said, my Mama always wanted the last word. So here you go, Mama. It's all yours.

Thanks, Mark.

When Daddy and I prayed, we had no idea how wonderfully God would answer our prayers. You are not only my favorite comedian but more than that, my heart is blessed and thankful when I see you ministering to families and children. As Ephesians says, God has truly done exceedingly abundant above all that we asked or thought according to his power and unto him be all the glory.

I love you with all my heart and I thank God for letting me be your mother.

Mama

Thanks, Mama.
Ooops. Sorry.
Guess I got the last word after all!

The End